THAT THEY MAY BE ONE?

The Episcopal-United Methodist Dialogue

C. FRANKLIN BROOKHART & GREGORY V. PALMER, CO-EDITORS

Seabury Books
NEW YORK

Cover design by Laurie Klein Westhafer
Typeset by Denise Hoff

Library of Congress Cataloging-in-Publication Data

A catalog record of this book is available from the Library of Congress.

ISBN-13: 978-1-59627-260-6 (pbk.)
ISBN-13: 978-1-59627-261-3 (ebook)

Seabury Books
19 East 34th Street
New York, New York 10016

www.churchpublishing.org

An imprint of Church Publishing Incorporated

Printed in the United States of America

CONTENTS

PREFACE

W HEN I ENGAGE in meaningful work with Christians of traditions other than my own I feel nearer to the heart of the triune God. It is not because this kind of work and engagement is easy. And God knows that it is not speedy. But I have no lack of conviction that every Christian is called to this work. John 17:21 says ". . . that they may all be one. As you, Father, are in me and I am in you, may they also be in us, so that the world may believe that you have sent me." Seeking to incarnate our essential oneness is not one of the heart prayers of our Lord Jesus Christ because it would be a nice thing if it could happen. The text from John more than intimates that this is an evangelistic yearning. To the end that we grow closer to one another in mission and ministry we convey to the world a sign of hope and healing.

The dialogue between the Episcopal Church and the United Methodist Church is one of these signs of hope and healing for our respective churches, the church beyond our denominations and the world. Already our dialogue has borne the fruit. My Episcopal counterpart and co-chair of the dialogue, Bishop Franklin Brookhart of the Diocese of Montana, in his introduction to this volume mentions, for example, a Theological Foundation document. In 2006 the dialogue produced *Make Us One with Christ* with an accompanying study guide to assist people from our two churches to come to know one another better. Another fruitful undertaking but not widely known or engaged reality is that our two churches are as we speak in Interim Eucharistic Sharing.

I am grateful to Nancy Bryan of Church Publishing for her vision for this book and her belief that it could be one more tool to help further learning and understanding of and among Episcopalians and United Methodists. You will find the essays provocative, challenging, and hopeful. They don't especially settle anything or everything but are but one more step in deepening the conversation and going to another level of honesty.

The Reverend Taylor Burton-Edwards, director of worship resources for the General Board of Discipleship of the United Methodist Church, has contributed an important essay focusing on the "distinctive flavors" of our respective worship traditions and practices. Most assuredly distinct flavors do not mean mutually exclusive flavors.

Bishop William B. Oden, now retired, is the former United Methodist co-chair of the dialogue. The work begun is still of great interest to him. He graciously labored to help this work by contributing an essay on the historic episcopate and its relationship to the dialogue and the goal of full communion. He offers some historical and practical guidance in going forward so that this important element need not be a "deal breaker."

Bishop Hope Morgan Ward is the resident bishop of the North Carolina Conference of the United Methodist Church. From 2004 to 2012 she served as the United Methodist bishop of Mississippi. It is out of this context that she offers "An Emerging Vision," which talks about shared worship, witness, and service of United Methodists and Episcopalians in Mississippi. Her Episcopal counterpart at the time, Bishop Duncan Gray, is also a contributor to this book.

This work is commended to you for reading, reflection, and conversation as the Episcopal Church and the United Methodist Church continue to journey together. I hope for its wide use for the sake of deepened conversation and shared witness. Without apology I will continue to gratefully work for full communion for our two churches. I pray without ceasing for the wide fulfillment of the prayer of Jesus in John 17:21.

†Gregory Vaughn Palmer

INTRODUCTION

Y ou have before you a collection of essays that comment on "A Theological Foundation for Full Communion between The Episcopal Church and The United Methodist Church." I hope these essays will aid your understanding and spark discussion about the possibility of full communion between these two churches.

"A Theological Foundation" represents years of work by the Episcopal-United Methodist Dialogue Team, and is offered as an extensive theological justification for proceeding with full communion between our two churches. The opening paragraph carefully defines full communion, stating what it is—mutual recognition and cooperation—and what it is not—organic merger. I believe it is a serious document requiring serious attention by members of both church bodies.

This book contains eight essays by eight members of The Episcopal Church. Dr. Bruce Mullin, professor of church history and world mission in the SPRL Chair and professor of modern Anglican studies at the General Theological Seminary in New York and also a member of the dialogue team, has written an introductory history of the Episcopalians and Methodists in the United States. As you read his work you will sense the crucial role history and context have played in developing the situation in which our two churches find themselves today. Dr. Mullin paints in broad strokes and properly prepares readers for studying "A Theological Foundation."

The Very Reverend Dr. Thomas Ferguson, dean of Bexley Hall Seminary in Columbus, Ohio, and staff advisor to the dialogue, presents a history of the dialogue itself. He first sets the workings of the dialogue in a larger context, and then narrates the work of the team from its beginning in 2002.

The Reverend Dr. Patrick Malloy, Porter Professor of Liturgics at the General Theological Seminary in New York City, responds to the document's statements about Holy Baptism, real presence in the Eucharist, and the issue of "open table." His work clarifies these important issues and pushes both churches toward further discussion and more clarity.

The Right Reverend Dr. William O. Gregg addresses issues of historic episcopate, presidency at the Eucharist, and the ministry of the laity. Bishop Gregg has served as bishop of Eastern Oregon and more recently as assisting bishop of North Carolina. He presents us with a probing essay that, in the end, raises the basic issue of what we can expect of ecumenical dialogues and what we hope to accomplish with full communion. He powerfully demonstrates that even careful theological work may not represent a sufficient basis for full communion, and that we, therefore, may need to address foundational issues in a new manner.

Because Bishop Gregg's critique is so important and extensive, the Reverend Dr. Ellen Wondra, professor of theology and ethics and academic dean at Seabury-Western Theological Seminary in Chicago and a widely known ecumenist, has been asked to respond to Bishop Gregg. The two essays should be considered together.

I have written the next essay, which addresses internal issues. I have in part set the issues within our American context and within the workings of the dialogue team.

The Rt. Rev. Duncan Gray, bishop of Mississippi, tells the story of the cooperation between his diocese and the United Methodist Conference. It is an encouraging and powerful narrative.

The concluding essay by Episcopalians comes from the Right Reverend Philip Duncan, bishop of the Central Gulf Coast. Bishop Duncan is also a member of the dialogue team and is chair of the church's Standing Committee on Ecumenism and Interreligious Relations. He sounds a rallying cry for both churches to live into the possibilities of full communion.

I wish to thank the co-editor of this volume and the co-chair of the dialogue, Bishop Gregory V. Palmer of the West Ohio Conference of the United Methodist Church. He joins me in praying that this book will advance the mission of God in our country and in the future ministries of our two churches.

†*C. Franklin Brookhart*

CHAPTER 1

Methodists and Episcopalians in American History

Robert Bruce Mullin

Methodists and Episcopalians have long been seen as "sibling" churches. They both are children of the eighteenth-century Church of England. But they are sibling churches with a difference. They have been siblings separated at birth, responding in fundamentally different ways to the new American environment. Our churches had different concepts of what was needed in this new American situation. For this reason it has only been in the last forty years that we have begun to recognize our family similarities.

Background

To understand Episcopalians and Methodists we must remember that both are products of post-1660 Restoration Anglicanism. For the first hundred-plus years of the organization of the Church of England there had been a furious debate over to what extent the English church should follow the model of the continental Protestant (i.e., Reformed or Calvinistic) churches. The Puritan/Anglican debate and the English Civil Wars were the culmination of this conflict. The post-1660 Restoration settlement shaped a normative Anglicanism from which Episcopalians and Methodists would both emerge and react to.

The most foundational element of this settlement was the established nature of the church. The church was the church by law established. In the Book of Common Prayer (BCP) of 1662 the martyrdom of King Charles I was lamented and the succession of Charles II was celebrated.

1

All clergy were to swear fealty to the crown, the book, and the establishment itself.

A second point was the centrality of episcopacy. During the previous century much of the Anglican/Puritan debate had concerned
the office of the episcopacy. Puritans (following Geneva) argued that
Presbyterianism was the true biblical polity. The Puritan-dominated
Long Parliament of the 1640s accordingly eliminated the Episcopal
office. At the time of the Restoration not only was the episcopacy
restored, but the ordination service revised. The ordinal of 1550 was
ambiguous as to whether episcopal ordination was necessary for ministration in the Church of England. The BCP of 1662 was explicit that
"Episcopal Consecration or Ordination" was a prerequisite for ministry
in the Church of England. But disagreement remained about the place
of this office. The "Preface to the Ordinal" merely stated "from the
Apostles' time there have been these Orders of Ministers in Christ's
Church; Bishops, Priests, and Deacons" and left it at that. Hence there
emerged a fundamental division between "high church" and ""low
church" Anglicans. High church persons believed that episcopacy was
part of the essence (*esse*) of the church. A church without bishops was
not a church. Accordingly they began to distance themselves from continental Protestants. "Low church" Anglicans thought that episcopacy
was only part of the well ordering (*bene esse*) of the church. A church
could be a church (though in an inferior state) without the presence of
bishops.

A third point may be called "Prayer Book" spirituality. The BCP
called for the regular recitation of certain prayers, and set forth a rhythm
of piety that shaped the day, the week, and the year. Undergirding this
was an understanding of Christianization that emphasized the accumu-
lation of holy habits brought about by these regular actions. Its premise
might be stated as "by doing we become." Religious action helped shape
the soul. This stood in contrast to the Puritan emphasis upon a religious life that began with the transformed heart. Puritans had criticized
the Elizabethan settlement for not emphasizing the state of the soul.
Without the right spirit, they argued, religious action was a sham. Only
by becoming could we do. Restoration Anglicanism, on the whole,
rejected such claims. Because of this piety they valued the physical place
of worship. A solemn location enhanced the dignity of worship, which
in turn made it more efficacious. Prayer Book spirituality, accordingly,
assumed the parochial system of the Church of England at the end of
the seventeenth century.

A fourth principle was an emphasis upon moderation, and a suspicion of enthusiasm. The Restoration saw the large-scale collapse of Calvinism in the Church of England, and the triumph of the free-will theories of Arminianism. Anglicans were convinced that the great destructiveness of the English Civil Wars and the Commonwealth period flowed from religious fanaticism. The Commonwealth was the age of Levellers, Diggers, Ranters, Quakers, et al, each believing that they were called by God to do their actions. Enthusiasm was the source of religious discord and social disruption. Likewise there was a belief that there were levels of religious assuredness. To its critics Puritanism advocated a rigid dogmatism of absolutes. Restoration Anglicans suggested that there were areas of gray, which the church must acknowledge and live with.

Such were some key emphases in the Restoration church. We might also note that Restoration Anglicanism saw two of its chief tasks as inculcating Christian morality and defending revealed religion against its critics. The first was viewed as important because of a perceived decline in morality as a result of the social dislocations of the Commonwealth period. The second became important in the face of the rise of Deism that questioned both biblical revelation and basic Christian doctrines.

Colonial Anglicans inherited these traditions. They saw themselves as part of the larger English church. The connection with the English church increased by the end of the seventeenth century. The bishop of London began to exercise enlarged governance through personal representatives, known as "commissaries." Also, in 1701 the Society for the Propagation of the Gospel (SPG) was established and began to send high church missionaries loyal to the crown to the colonies. But if colonial Anglicans shared this Restoration heritage, there were regional variations. In the southern colonies the church was established. Southern churchmen saw the role of the church to be the upholder of reason, order, and an ordered morality. Lay persons had distinctive influence there, so the clerical nature of the church was kept in check. Conversely in the northern colonies, where in many ways the church was made up of converts, the distinctiveness of Anglicanism, and particularly the office of the episcopacy, came to be heralded.

Wesley's Revolution

John Wesley had a distinct relationship with this Restoration Anglicanism. He was a faithful cleric in the Church of England (and indeed originally received the tag "Methodist" because he was so methodical in observing the practices of the Church of England). But by the late 1730s he became dissatisfied with Prayer Book piety. As it is famously known, Wesley's heart was "strangely warmed" at the Aldersgate Street chapel in 1738. Wesley's emphasis upon the transformed heart was a protest against the piety of the Prayer Book as an end in itself. It was part of a larger pietistic movement that emphasized that true religion was of the heart, and not simply the head. As he stated in his "An Earnest Appeal to Men of Reason and Religion," a religion of church, prayer, sacrament, fasting, holy reading, etc., was of no value without the inner working of the Spirit.[1] Wesley was an Arminian in this claim. God wanted all to be saved, and it was the responsibility of the preacher to set forth the word of salvation. Wesley offered other innovations such as an itinerant ministry and class meetings, involving small groups for edification and encouragement. Itinerancy allowed Wesley to address failures in the English parochial system, caused by a population shifting from villages to cities. Class meetings allowed for both the inculcating of a warm-hearted religion, and also the addressing of questions of morality, particularly the abuse of alcohol. But Wesley saw his as a reform or revival movement in the Church of England, and not as a separate body.

Beginning in the 1740s the American religious scene began to be reshaped by the forces of the Great Awakening. The Great Awakening can be broadly seen as the American equivalent of the Wesley revival of England. Both movements emphasized this new religious understanding known as Evangelicalism. Wesley's associate, George Whitefield, was the great proponent of it on both sides of the Atlantic. Evangelical, or conversion oriented, piety became increasingly popular throughout the eighteenth century, but colonial Anglican churches, on the whole, rejected it. Anglican lay people, however, did not. Large segments of southern Anglican laity began to be attracted to the new message. They seemed to find the established southern churches lacking in warmth and vigor. But there were few clergy to support their yearnings. This lay response became the seedbed for the growth of American Methodism. Methodist lay preachers began to emerge in the 1760s (particularly in the Chesapeake environ), and by the early 1770s Wesley began sending preachers to the new world, most famously Francis Asbury. But, just as in England, these preachers shared Wesley's fealty to the established church, and saw themselves as strengthening colonial Anglicanism.

---

1 "An Earnest Appeal to Men of Reason and Religion," in *John Wesley*, Albert C. Outler, ed. (New York: Oxford University Press, 1964), 400.

The Challenge of the American Revolution

The revolutionary era was vexing for both colonial Anglicans and Methodists. The northern Anglican campaign to establish an American episcopate engendered strong opposition from English-speaking Protestants who associated episcopacy with the earlier policies of the high church Archbishop of Canterbury William Laud. Many Anglican clergy in the north, in contrast, heard the voice of militant Puritan Roundheads behind the colonial clamor against episcopacy. As the relationship between England and her colonies deteriorated, Anglican clergy faced a dilemma. Both in their liturgy and in their ordination promises they were tied to the king. Accordingly, many in the north chose the path of Loyalism, and upheld the case of the crown. When independence was proclaimed they found themselves in a difficult situation and many had to close their churches rather than violate their vows. In the southern colonies, the church was not linked to Loyalism, but the revolutionary spirit of the times quickly led to the eradication of the establishments in Virginia, Maryland, and other colonies. The flight of Loyalist laypersons to Canada and Britain weakened the church, as did the withdrawal of the SPG missionaries after the peace of Paris in 1783.

Methodists faced a similar problem. John Wesley himself was critical of the Revolution, and published works condemning it, such as "A Calm Address to our American Colonies." Loyalism also marked the Methodist missionaries. All, save Asbury, left the colonies after the declaration of independence. By the late 1770s Methodism was increasingly under the influence of lay preachers.

Bishops and Organization

By the early 1780s Anglicans and Methodists faced the question of reorganization, and different models emerged. William White of Philadelphia, in *The Case of the Episcopal Churches Considered*, called for a reorganization of the church around Republican principles. Reorganization meant the necessity of providing ordained clergy, and until the situation with England was normalized, he called for presbyterial ordination to establish "conditional" ministers. For him episcopacy was merely part of the *bene esse* of the church. Samuel Seabury and the clergy of Connecticut, in contrast, believed episcopacy was essential and had to precede any church organization. Hence in 1783 they elected Seabury bishop and sent him to England to receive consecration from the English bishops. When it became clear for political reasons that no such consecration was to be had, he turned to the Scottish Episcopal Church (which the Church of England did not recognize) for Episcopal consecration. From the twenty-first century perspective it is easy to ignore how revolutionary Seabury's action was. It broke the longstanding American subservience to the English church. Both White and Seabury were forced to set forth plans for church organization that were radical breaks from the earlier English tradition.

Wesley faced a similar dilemma. With the treaty of Paris he recognized that American Methodists could no longer be part of the Church of England, and would need to be organized as a separate church. Whereas combing Anglicanism and Methodism in the established Church of England was conceivable to him, such a combination was almost impossible after the colonies had become independent. Frustrated by the refusal of the bishop of London to ordain Methodist preachers for America, he invoked the principle of presbyterial ordination, citing as his authority both the practice of the ancient church of Alexandria and the writings of Lord Peter King on the primitive church. In 1784 he ordained Thomas Coke to be superintendent of the church in America. Wesley, too, believed that the critical times called for bold innovation.

Models of Organization

The immediate years after 1783 were a period of organization for both Episcopalians and Methodists, and in these organizations one sees key divergences that would shape the two communions.

Largely through the efforts of William White, a General Convention was called for September of 1785 with the task of organizing a national church. A constitution was drafted, the revision of the liturgy was begun, and the process of negotiating with the Church of England for the extension of the episcopacy was undertaken. The constitution attempted to carefully balance the rights of clergy and laity, and the liturgy included some new innovations as well as the restoration of older forms.

This process was largely completed by 1789 when Samuel Seabury and his churches united with General Convention. In all of this process, continuity with the English church was stressed. The preface to the Book of Common Prayer stated, "this Church is far from intending to depart from the Church of England in any essential point of doctrine, discipline or worship; or further than local circumstances require." The liturgy and constitution were offered to the English bishops for their inspection and were revised in light of English reaction. A similar principle, found in both the constitution and the first canons, was the centrality of the office of the bishop and the Book of Common Prayer. No person could officiate in a church without episcopal ordination, and no prayers could be used that were not to be found in the official liturgy. Still a third point of continuity with the Church of England was an insistence on a learned clergy, which meant knowledge of Greek and Latin. This care bespoke a general attitude among Episcopalians at the time. Having been transformed as a result of the Revolution from an established (or at the very least imperial) church into a small minority status community, the first concern was to make sure order, identity, and continuity were maintained. In this vein the model of worship as parochial was maintained.

The situation among Methodists was quite different. American Methodists organized at the "Christmas Conference" of 1784. John Wesley exercised considerable personal authority over British Methodists, and assumed the same among his American followers. He sent to them Thomas Coke to be superintendent with a commission to ordain Asbury the same; a revised liturgy based on the English Book of Common Prayer; a church polity that positioned the threefold ministry within the operative Methodist Book of Discipline; a hymnbook; and a reduced number of Articles of Religion (one must here note that Episcopalians in the 1790s considered pruning the Articles before adopting them in 1801). But American Methodists immediately exercised a spirit of independence. Coke was not received but elected (along with Francis Asbury) by the Conference. The authority of the Conference and not personal authority was to govern Methodism, and it was to have ultimate authority. Likewise, much to Wesley's consternation, Coke and Asbury soon claimed the title "bishop" and not superintendent. And they began the process (completed in 1792) of rejecting Wesley's liturgy. The sacramental rites, occasional offices, and revised Articles of Religion were incorporated into the Book of Discipline (Methodism's central document), but the liturgy as such was not. The idea of reading prescribed prayers offended the sensibilities of many Methodist preachers who as pietists saw the heart of religion to be the relationship of the individual with God. Unlike Episcopalians who believed that liturgical uniformity was key to survival in the new environment, Methodists opted for freedom of worship. They also adopted the "itinerant principle" allowing for ministry freed from parish bounds. Finally they affirmed the principle of "connectionalism" in which Methodist preachers would gather annually for governance and encouragement. All of these things gave a spirit of independence and innovation and showed comparatively little interest in continuity. It is noteworthy that while Episcopalians took care to record their organization procedures, Methodists neglected to keep minutes of either the Christmas Conference or their first General Conference (1792).

Episcopal historians speak of the events of the 1780s as the "great compromise" bringing together the low church South and the high church North into one united church, but they often ignore that what was lost from colonial Anglicanism was the Methodist community. Episcopalians were too preoccupied with their internal concerns to reach out to the fledgling Methodist community. Not that there were no attempts. In 1791 Thomas Coke wrote to William White about the possibility of union. He noted, however, two concerns that stood in the way, and both reflect diverging views of the role of the church in the new society. The first concerned the ministers ordained by Coke and Asbury, who would not give up the right to administer sacraments. The second concerned Methodist preachers, who would not surrender their right to preach even though they did not know biblical languages.[2] Both regular ordination and a learned clergy were considered normative for Anglican clergy at the time, but Coke called for latitude in the name of mission. Nothing came of the request, and Methodists and Episcopalians went on in their separate ways.

Relating to the New Republic

The adaptations Methodists embraced in the 1780s put them in good stead to respond to the religious needs of the young republic. As Americans poured across the Appalachian Mountains and the culture began moving towards an individualistic market economy, the old parochial model of Christianization seemed not to fit. This is the period scholars have called the Second Great Awakening. They speak of the triumph of a "vernacular" form of theology and preaching, much less elite and rather tied to the common people. Here Methodists excelled. Their activism, innovation, and connectional order became keys to their success. Two institutions in particular were critical in Christianizing the trans–Appalachian west. One was the camp meeting, or protracted periods of preaching that emphasized heart religion and conversion over refined theology. This proved ideal for Methodists, who thrived in the rough–and–tumble world. The second was the circuit rider system in which preachers would

---

2 The correspondence is found in William White, *Memoirs of the Protestant Episcopal Church in the United States of America* (New York, 1836), 343–348.

be given a circuit of congregations to which to minister. No individual congregation could support a cleric, but through the work of circuit riders vast numbers of persons were ministered to. The period from 1790 to 1840 saw tremendous Methodist growth. By 1840, Methodism was the largest Christian denomination in America, claiming 34 percent of church membership. Scholars have called this the "Methodist Age" of American religion, and have noted that by 1840 there were more Methodist churches in America than there were post offices! Other groups, such as the Baptists, also flourished in this environment, and by 1840 the old colonial denominations had but a fraction of the religious populace compared to the "popular" churches. This period of rapid growth would leave its mark upon American Methodism. Church growth was seen as a visible sign of divine blessing. Furthermore, this growth was transforming the soul of the nation.

Episcopalians did not on the whole participate in this vast religious expansion. The years of remarkable Methodist growth saw the Episcopal Church still trying to find its sea legs in the new republic. Disestablishment virtually brought to ruins the once proud colonial church of Virginia, and in many parts of the country the rebuilding was slow. It was not until the second decade of the nineteenth century that signs of vitality began to appear. Much of this had to do with a revival of churchmanship which vivified large groups of Episcopalians. In places like New York, John Henry Hobart emphasized the "high church" nature of the Episcopal Church. Apostolic succession linked Episcopalians to the primitive church and differentiated it from all other American Protestants. It was the responsibility of Episcopalians to emphasize its distinctive teachings and to avoid collaboration with other Protestant communities, including Methodists.

In Massachusetts and Virginia there emerged a form of Anglican evangelicalism advocating the preaching of the cross, the transformed heart, and a rigorous personal piety. Since Anglican Evangelicalism had its roots in the same eighteenth-century stirring of piety that gave birth to Methodism, one might think that they and Methodists would have shared much in common, but that was not the case. On both key theological and cultural points differences prevented a closer rapprochement with Methodism. On the theological level, Anglican Evangelicalism was Calvinistic rather than Arminian. It tended therefore to see itself associated more with Presbyterianism than with Arminian Methodism. Many of its leaders were trained at places like Princeton and adopted key element of the Princeton theology. This closeness to Presbyterianism was not merely because of theology. Episcopalians and Presbyterians occupied the same social location. They both advocated a learned ministry, and favored a refined culture. They both ministered (albeit not exclusively) to educated and professional laity. Methodism (at least in antebellum America) was largely outside of their orbit. It was usually grouped as one of the "popular" churches and had strong populist and democratic elements. Episcopalians did not see themselves as one of the "popular" churches. For both high and low Episcopalians one does not find the centrality of growth language that was so present in Methodism. As a result of the revolutionary period Episcopalians acknowledged that theirs was to be a comparatively small church whose influence was to be social and cultural and not democratic or populist.

Still another cultural difference separated Episcopalians and Methodists. The trauma of the revolutionary period left the Episcopal Church small and comparatively weak. As a result of this, the importance of church unity became paramount. In the Great Litany the devout asked to be delivered "from all false doctrine, heresy, and schism," and particularly the last mentioned was taken seriously. Even though there were at times often violent clashes between high and low church Episcopalians, church unity was maintained. This was not the case among Methodists. Doctrinal and other differences often led some Methodists to split off from the mother body. The breaking away of the Methodist Protestant Church in 1830 is but one example. Truth was to be cherished more than church unity.

Slavery and Division

These different attitudes profoundly shaped the churches' differing responses to the issues of slavery and secession. John Wesley had been strongly anti-slavery and early Methodism had been rigorous in excluding slave holders or dealers from membership. But as Methodists took root in the south, toleration of slavery and slave holders became the rule. As abolitionist fervor rose in the north in the 1830s this compromise was no longer seen as tolerable. In 1844 the Methodists divided north and south over the question of slavery. And it was not a pretty division. Conflicts raged in some states over where the border lay between the two churches, and the question of dividing the assets of the publishing concerns ultimately had to be decided by the Supreme Court.

In contrast, American Episcopalians, on the official level, were silent on the question of slavery. Slavery was potentially a church-dividing issue (as it had divided Presbyterians and Baptists as well as Methodists), and Episcopalians would not be divided. Indeed in 1859, General

Convention, which normally met in a northern city such as New York or Philadelphia, met in Richmond, Virginia, hoping to show a dividing nation how the church could be an example of harmonial unity.

When war came southern and northern Methodists became vigorous supporters of their regional cause. Episcopalians were more ambivalent about the war. Southern Episcopalians argued that they were not committing schism by organizing in a southern Episcopal Church, rather they were compelled to by the course of political events. They expressed no bitterness towards their northern colleagues. In the north, Episcopalians responded to the war with an initial coolness. Unlike northern Methodists (as well as Congregationalists, Baptists, and Presbyterians) they did not immediately embrace the war effort. Although in 1862 (through pressure by the Lincoln administration) they formally endorsed the war, they refused to condemn southern Episcopalians as schismatics. Because of this the Episcopal Church reunited with comparative ease after the war. In contrast the ill will between northern and southern Methodists would keep them separated until 1939.

In the decades after the Civil War both churches attempted to respond to the plight of the freed slaves (albeit paying little attention to each other). Both Episcopalians and northern Methodists through various denominational organizations reached out to the new free black community. Both churches founded educational institutions in the southern states. Southern Methodists preferred to encourage black Methodists to create a separate denomination, and in 1870 the Colored Methodist Church was founded. Despite these actions Methodists and Episcopalians lost many of their pre-war black members.

Lingering Methodist Issues

If issues of churchmanship divided nineteenth-century American Episcopalians, the issue of plainness versus respectability divided Methodists. From the very beginning there had been a subtle tension in American Methodism. On the one hand there was the celebration of plainness. Just as early Methodists eschewed a learned ministry in favor of heartfelt preachers, so too did they look with disfavor on the pomp and luxury associated with much church worship. But they always respected education. In 1789 the Methodist Book Concern was established to produce literature for its preachers, and this was the earliest denominational publishing house in America. Education was part of character, and leaders such as Nathan Bangs labored to use education as a tool to improve the character of American Methodism. This led to the founding of a series of colleges such as what is now Wesleyan University in 1831. Likewise, as Methodists grew in prosperity many no longer found the diatribes against artistry persuasive. In 1855 Christ Church Pittsburgh built the first neo-Gothic church building in American Methodism. In the years after the Civil War, as the social status of Methodists continued to rise, this trend would continue and American Methodists established the largest group of universities in the American Protestant world. Even such scholarly churches as the Presbyterians (not to mention Episcopalians, who established comparatively few colleges and only one university) could not compete with the Methodist effort. But these trends created tensions among those Methodists who believed such moves towards education and refinement were sacrificing the original spirit of the movement.

This tension also had a theological component. One of Wesley's distinctive teachings was the idea of Christian holiness, or a belief in a supernatural experience that followed conversion and thereby empowered a believer to triumph over sin. Believing that this teaching was passing away, some Methodists in 1867 established the "National Camp Meeting for the Promotion of Holiness." By the 1880s tensions between holiness Methodists and others became so great that holiness advocates began to withdraw and form their own denominations, such as the Church of the Nazarene. Eventually from this separation would emerge the movement known as Pentecostalism.

Late Nineteenth-Century Themes

The postwar enthusiasm for mission led each church to redouble its missionary endeavor both at home and abroad. These missionary efforts were crucially supported by women (both formally and informally). Leaders such as the Methodists' Isabella Thoburn and Lucy Rider Myer and the Episcopalians' Mary Abbot Emery Twing and Julia Chester Emery did much to encourage missions. These efforts led to great growth in both churches. The number of Episcopalians increased from 1 in 416 Americans in 1830 to 1 in 95 in 1906. Methodist growth was even more impressive. Methodist churches were being constructed at a rate of two a day and some Methodists gleefully changed the line of the hymn "All Hail the Power of Jesus' Name" to "All hail the power of Jesus' name; we are building two a day." Both churches also engaged in ministry to Native Americans.

But new intellectual changes proved more problematic. *The Origin of Species*, written by Charles Darwin in 1859, and the importation of the higher biblical criticism coming out of Germany created problems for the old theology and piety. Although many Methodists and Episcopalians felt threatened, others tried to reach an understanding. Boston University School of Theology and the Episcopal Theological School of Cambridge, Massachusetts, became centers for the reconciliation of the old religion with the new science and history. But even here the responses showed different starting points for Episcopalians and Methodists. Drawing from their sacramental tradition some Episcopalians used the doctrine of the incarnation to link God to the world. In contrast, the Methodist theologians stressed the importance of personal religious experience. Borden Parker Bowne of Boston University offered a Boston "personalism" that posited the human personality as the starting point of Christian theology.

Still another challenge was the new social world of the cities. American cities provided a twofold problem for Protestant Christians. In the urban social divisions between rich and poor, many on the bottom were left with inadequate housing, insecure employment, little medical resources, and other pressing needs. Secondly, these cities were becoming increasingly filled with immigrants who had little if anything in common with the Anglo-Saxon religious tradition. Episcopalians and Methodists in turn responded, but they responded out of their own heritages.

The first attempt by Episcopalians was to make the church more inclusive. The institutional church movement attempted to extend the ministry of the church to all aspects of a person's life—providing medical dispensaries, classes on cooking and cleaning, various clubs—in order to make the church useful. These endeavors helped to introduce foreign persons to the new urban American context. Secondly, there was a recognition that the liturgy needed to be more flexible to meet this new population. In the first decade of the twentieth century the constitution was changed to allow for some liturgical flexibility recognizing the need for variations in foreign language translations. In addition, individual Episcopalians came together in organizations such as the Church Association for the Advancement of the Interest of Labor (C.A.I.L.) to advocate social reform.

Methodists, in contrast, were far more organizational in their responses. In 1905 the Methodist Federation for Social Services was established, and three years later (1908) northern Methodists adopted a Social Creed, calling for the abolition of child labor and the sweating system and other social reforms. Methodists became the first Protestant church to adopt such a formal creed. Methodist reformers also provided important leadership in the late nineteenth-century campaign against alcoholic beverages, which culminated in the passing of national prohibition in 1919. Episcopalians were less unified in the crusade against alcohol.

The differing attitudes of the churches can be seen in how they chose to make their presence known in the nation's capital. In 1920 Methodist bishop William F. McDowell called for a distinctive Methodist presence in the nation's capital. "The Board of Temperance, Prohibition and Public Morals has the perfect site and the perfect plans. . . . The new building will make our church visible and multiply its power at this world's center." In 1923 Methodists dedicated this new building (the Methodist Building) to house among other groups the Methodist Federation for Social Services. It was to be the center of Methodist attempts to influence public policy. In contrast Episcopalians decided to construct a national cathedral. Episcopal presence would be through prayer and ceremony.

Also during these years Episcopalians and Methodists began to connect with their non-American co-religionists. In 1867, at the invitation of the archbishop of Canterbury, the first Lambeth Conference was called, bringing together bishops from around the Anglican world. The Lambeth Conference would continue to meet every ten years (except at times of war) for discussion and fellowship. In 1881 the Ecumenical Methodist Conference (now the World Methodist Council) first met in London, bringing together thirty Methodist bodies from twenty countries. It too has continued to meet every ten years.

Entering the Twentieth Century

In the twentieth century both Episcopalians and Methodists responded to the call for ecumenism to reunite the divided body of Christ. The Edinburgh Missionary Conference of 1910 awakened many to the scandal of a divided Christendom. But here, as elsewhere, Episcopalians and Methodists responded out of their own cultures.

From as early as the middle of the nineteenth century some American Episcopalians saw their church as the foundation for a larger church unity. In 1853 William A. Muhlenberg and others issued a memorial calling for the extension of apostolic (i.e., episcopally ordained) ministry to other churches. More importantly, in 1873 William R. Huntington published *The Church-Idea*, calling for a uniting of all Protestant churches on four principals: scripture, creeds, the two sacraments, and the historic episcopate. Huntington's call was taken up and eventually enshrined in the Lambeth Quadrilateral of 1888, which became the foundation of Anglican ecumenical theory. What marked the Anglican vision was the idea of ecclesial union. Cooperative union in life and work, Charles Brent would argue, was not enough. We must move unto unity in faith and order.

American Episcopalians attempted two great ecumenical endeavors in the first half of the twentieth century. In 1919 a concordat was proposed to unite Episcopalians and Congregationalists, while in 1946 another concordat called for the uniting of Episcopalians and Presbyterians. Both failed. Significantly, however, Episcopalians chose as their potential ecumenical partners not churches that were part of their same liturgical or theological family, but those who inhabited the same social and cultural world. There was no talk of reaching out to Methodists.

Methodists in turn poured the bulk of their ecumenical labor into repairing nineteenth-century divisions. These efforts culminated in 1939 with the reunion of northern and southern Methodists as well as the Methodist Protestant Church. This concern for family unity would be further extended in 1968 with the uniting of Methodists and Evangelical United Brethren (a historically German communion) to create the United Methodist Church. The 1939 union came with a price, however. It placed African American Methodists in a "Central Jurisdiction," and in the decades to follow African American Methodists saw themselves as second-class citizens in the Methodist family.

Both churches endured the stresses and challenges of the first decades of the twentieth century. Both fervently embraced the allied cause in the First World War, and both pondered the social changes of the 1920s. Methodists, in particular, were forced to grapple with the fact that their cherished social reform of prohibition proved to be unsuccessful, and in some circles led to scorn towards its advocates. Likewise each church was forced to grapple with the crisis of the Great Depression which sapped economic resources, and called into question the health of a capitalist America. The crisis made socially active Methodists even more critical of the economic order. Some Episcopalians, in turn, saw in Franklin D. Roosevelt (an Episcopal vestryman) and his New Deal an Episcopal solution to the crisis of the times, but probably the majority of people in the pews did not follow.

Both Methodists and Episcopalians benefitted from the surge of prosperity and piety following the end of the Second World War. Both churches engaged in extensive church-building as Americans began to move from cities to suburbs. One downside of this migration was that great inner-city churches, which had been the jewels of the denominations, found themselves being transformed into albatrosses. But new churches also increased demands for ministry and new seminaries were established by both denominations.

The postwar years began to show seeds of a conservative/liberal tension in both churches. In the face of the Cold War clergy and laity began to see the world somewhat differently. Methodist (and to a lesser extent Episcopal) clergy saw the future to lay with world government and peaceful coexistence, hence they tried to downplay conflicts between east and west. Many of the laity were less optimistic and embraced the rhetoric of the Cold War. It was a minor issue but would not go away.

Certain intellectual trends provided a common ground for Methodists and Episcopalians for the first time in 160 years. The university divinity schools (many under Methodist auspice) allowed for Methodists and Episcopalians to discover each other, particularly at the advanced degree level. Places like Duke, Emory, and Boston became early centers of informal Episcopal/Methodist dialogue. These schools also were arenas where a new ecumenical spirit took root academically. Scholars reopened issues of longstanding division, and tried, if possible, to get behind the earlier stalemates. The gradual shift in Episcopal language from "apostolic succession" to "historic episcopate" is a case in point. Apostolic succession implied an exclusivity, and that there was only one way to be connected with the apostolic church. "Historic episcopate" was a broader category. These and other explorations laid the groundwork for the later ecumenical document "Baptism, Eucharist, and Ministry" (BEM) which saw in these sacramental actions the center of a united church.

Likewise the emergence of the liturgical movement after the Second World War would shape the churches. One may date the rediscovery of ritual among Methodists to Nolan Harmon's 1926 *Rites and Rituals of Episcopal Methodism*. But the postwar movement pushed both churches further. It impressed upon Episcopalians that the issue of liturgy was broader than the study of the prayer books of Thomas Cranmer. Methodists began to see less conflict between gospel worship and liturgical practice. Most importantly, both communions began to recognize that a passion liturgy was not backward-looking, but something that enriched and formed Christian communities.

Finally, a revival of Wesleyan studies in the scholarship and advocacy of Frank Baker and Albert Outler began to reclaim the "Anglican" world of John Wesley. Attention to Charles (Wesley's brother) and Susannah (his mother) also aided that reclamation of the churchly Wesleys. The world of eighteenth-century Anglicanism began to be seen as common ground.

The New Challenges

The optimism and confidence of both churches was challenged by the events of the 1960s and beyond. During that decade, the "Protestant Era" of American life (which Methodists and Episcopalians did so much to support) began to crumble and neither church found itself in the center of things any longer. America was becoming a more secular place. Furthermore, new issues began to emerge that would prove to be daunting. One was race. The Civil Rights movement challenged the compromises these churches had made over race, both on the congregational level and above. The Central Jurisdiction that had marginalized Methodists of color was disbanded between 1967 and 1973. The General Convention of the Episcopal Church gave unprecedented concern for racial questions in 1967 and 1969. Still, racial issues continued to challenge both churches.

A second question was the role of women. Although women had for centuries made up the majority in the pews, their formal role was limited. Methodists had an easier time with this question. The admission of women to full clerical privileges in 1956 was accomplished with little controversy. For Episcopalians it was not so easy. Some high church Episcopalians feared that the ordination of women would threaten the catholic nature of the priesthood. The mid-1970s experienced an acrid debate, and the decision by General Convention in 1976 to allow for women's ordination was not universally praised. It would not be until 1987 that the episcopate would be opened to women. Even though the ministry of women has been accepted by the vast majority of Episcopalians (and seen as a blessing), a remnant of Episcopalians still refuse to accept these changes.

Finally, issues of gender have become one of the most controversial questions facing the two communions. When this question first arose in the 1970s it perplexed the churches. Whether gay and lesbian members could married in the church, and whether they could serve in ordained ministry (particularly the episcopacy), have become issues polarizing conservatives and liberals. Various Christian principles seemed in conflict over these questions.

Rediscovery

By the late 1980s Episcopalians and Methodists began to look at each other afresh and began to see real parallels. The failures of the great pan-Protestant ecumenical schemes for organic unity of the earlier decades (such as COCU and CUIC) led Methodist and Episcopal ecumenists to recognize that they had more in common with other episcopal churches than they had with non-episcopal churches. Both churches enthusiastically embraced both episcopacy and democracy, distinguishing them from non-episcopal Presbyterians and non-democratic Roman Catholics. The success of Lutheran/Episcopal unity through *Called to Common Mission* suggested a possible path for Methodists and Episcopalians. They began to look more closely at their liturgical and sacramental practices and question how each might learn from the other. Finally, they saw in each other the DNA of Restoration Anglicanism, in eschewing rigid dogmatism, and accepting the reality of gray areas as they tried to make their way into the future. Siblings, separated from birth, had found each other.

*Dr. Bruce Mullin is Professor of Church History
and World Mission in the SPRL Chair
and Professor of Modern Anglican Studies at the
General Theological Seminary in New York.
He has also served as a member of the
Episcopal-United Methodist Dialogue Team.*

CHAPTER 2

Caught in the Parent Trap: Anglicans and Methodists in the USA

Thomas Ferguson

The Parent Trap

A colleague of mine once likened the relationship between Methodists and Anglicans in the United States to the classic 1960s Disney film *The Parent Trap*. In that film, two siblings are separated at birth and grow up not knowing of one another's existence, living separate lives, unaware of their common past. While not a perfect analogy, it does capture some elements of the ways Episcopalians and Methodists have related to one another in the United States. Despite common roots in Anglicanism, Episcopalians and United Methodists in this country have largely lived separate ecclesial lives, beginning trajectories of separation in the eighteenth century that were deepened by divisions in race and socioeconomic class.

As the Episcopal Church and the United Methodist Church began to consider concrete proposals for sharing in ministry for the sake of common witness and mission, this introductory essay is designed to give an overview of the history of dialogue between these two communions, complementing other essays that go into depth on the historical development of Anglicanism and Methodism.

History of Dialogue

By the late 1780s, Episcopalians and Methodists had formally separated into new church bodies. Despite this, one of the first movements towards dialogue was birthed shortly after the formation of the Methodist Episcopal Church and the Protestant Episcopal Church in the United

States of America when Thomas Coke approached William White about the possibility of dialogue leading towards reunion. Coke wrote to White in 1791, lamenting the separation between Episcopalians and Methodists. He noted that Methodists in America has gone "further in the separation of our church than Mr. Wesley. . . did intend." Perhaps as an inducement for Episcopalians to be willing to incorporate Methodists into their new church, Coke stressed the growth and size of Methodism, citing membership numbers that already dwarfed the small and struggling Protestant Episcopal Church. Coke proposed the establishment of a structure for Methodists within the Episcopal Church (dare we say a kind of Methodist ordinariate?[1]) with its own bishops (one did not need many guesses to presume whom Coke had in mind to be these bishops):

> But if the two houses of the convention of the clergy[2] would consent to your consecration of Mr Asbury and me as bishops of the Methodist Society in the Protestant Episcopal Church in these United States (or by any title, if that not be proper), on the supposition of the reunion of these two churches, under proper mutual stipulations, and engage that the Methodist Society shall have a regular supply, on the death of their bishops, and so, *ad perpetuum*. . . [3]

It is important to note that this remained at this stage almost entirely a private exchange between White and Coke, and it is highly doubtful their broader communions would have shown much enthusiasm for any kind of reunion discussions. Coke himself noted to White that there would be significant resistance within the Methodist Episcopal Church, including from its only other bishop, Francis Asbury.

Events took a curious turn with the news of the death of John Wesley, which prompted Coke to try to return to England, in the hope of being chosen successor to Wesley in leading the British Methodist societies. On his way to find passage to England, he stopped in Philadelphia, where he met privately with White. Coke was surprised by White's willingness to

---

1 In the apostolic constitution *Anglicanorum Coetibus*, Pope Benedict XVI authorized the establishment of an ordinariate for groups of Anglicans seeking to enter into full communion with the Roman Catholic Church. For a description of one of these ordinariates, see http://www.usordinariate.org/.

2 Coke is presumably referring to the House of Deputies and House of Bishops, and seemed unaware that the House of Deputies included lay and clerical representatives.

3 Letter from Thomas Coke to Samuel Seabury, May 14, 1791. Quoted in E. Edward Beardsley, *The Life and Correspondence of the Rt Rev Samuel Seabury* (Boston: Houghton Mifflin, 1881), 400–401.

consider his proposal, with White suggesting that Episcopalians might consider ordaining Coke and Asbury as bishops for a Methodist structure within the Episcopal Church. Encouraged by this, Coke wrote to Samuel Seabury (who was the current presiding bishop) in May of 1791, pitched much the same proposal to him as he had to White, and then departed for England.[4] Just before his departure, however, he met with Asbury. Asbury knew of his overture to White and was opposed to it, and the rift between the two men deepened.

Coke's proposal was doomed from the beginning. It was only a personal initiative, with little support from other Methodists, including the only other bishop in America. White's initially positive response was likewise his own personal opinion, and sentiment against Methodism and the dangers of "enthusiasm" still ran deep. The exchange is indicative, in some ways, of how the issues of race and class would become significant factors in how Methodists and Anglicans related to one another. On the question of race, Coke was clear to point out the large number of African Americans who had joined the Methodist Episcopal Church and who would help increase the size of the Protestant Episcopal Church. On the question of class, Coke notes that an impediment to reunion would be the educational standards of Methodist clergy, hardly any of whom had formal theological training, in contrast to the high standards required in the Episcopal Church. Coke notes, for instance, that almost all the Methodists would have to be dispensed from the Greek and Latin proficiency requirements in the Episcopal Church's canons.[5] Anglicans and Methodists would not reach out to one another in formal dialogue for nearly a century.

The next efforts towards dialogue emerged in the 1880s, as the Episcopal Church formulated what would become known as the Chicago-Lambeth Quadrilateral. In 1886, the House of Bishops of the Episcopal Church adopted four points to be the foundation for seeking dialogue and deeper unity with other communions. In 1888, these four points were slightly modified by the Lambeth Conference of Bishops, the decennial gathering of all Anglican bishops in the world. Dialogue with other churches would be on the basis of the following, known as the Chicago-Lambeth Quadrilateral:

---

4 There is no known response by Seabury to Coke's letter.
5 For a history of the exchanges between Coke and White, see John Wigger, *American Saint: Francis Asbury and the Methodists* (New York: Oxford University Press, 2009), 195–199.

The Holy Scriptures of the Old and New Testaments, as "containing all things necessary to salvation," and as being the rule and ultimate standard of faith.

The Apostles' Creed, as the Baptismal Symbol; and the Nicene Creed, as the sufficient statement of the Christian faith.

The two Sacraments ordained by Christ Himself—Baptism and the Supper of the Lord—ministered with unfailing use of Christ's words of Institution, and of the elements ordained by Him.

The Historic Episcopate, locally adapted in the methods of its administration to the varying needs of the nations and peoples called of God into the Unity of His Church.

The Episcopal Church then reached out to a wide variety of Christian communions in the decades that followed, proposing dialogue on the basis of the Quadrilateral. There was limited response, though eventually there were substantive dialogues with the Congregational Church and later the United Presbyterian Church, resulting in proposals to the General Convention of the Episcopal Church in 1919 and 1943, respectively. The two largest Methodist churches declined the invitation, largely because of efforts towards reunion within the Methodist tradition. In 1939, the Methodist Church would be formed through the merger of the Methodist Episcopal Church; the Methodist Episcopal Church, South; and the Methodist Protestant Church. However, any dialogue that could have resulted following this merger was curtailed by the onset of the Second World War.

An ecumenical spring followed the conclusion of the Second World War. The World Council of Churches was formed in 1948 and the National Council of Churches of Christ in the United States in 1950, with the Methodist Church and Episcopal Church founding members of both. The first bilateral dialogue between Methodists and Episcopalians took place in the 1950s. Approved by the Methodist Church's General Conference and the General Convention of the Episcopal Church, the dialogue first met in November of 1953. At the April 1955 meeting of the dialogue the Episcopal Church made a proposal for "intercommunion," which would include "bringing the Methodist bishops within the historic episcopate."[6] Following the dialogue, a group of eleven

6 *Journal of the General Convention of the Protestant Episcopal Church in the United States of America* (1955), Report of the Joint Commission on Approaches to Unity, 657.

Episcopal bishops and eight Methodist bishops met to discuss the proposal, and reached "strong consensus" that such informal meetings of bishops between the two churches should continue. Conversations continued, with the proposal being "revised several times" over the next several years. Efforts were also made to better understand one another's churches, with Episcopalians noting that they had a "much clearer appreciation of the Methodist tradition and teaching."[7]

Getting to know one another better, however, seems to have had the opposite effect than intended, as enthusiasm for the draft proposal for intercommunion cooled considerably by the early 1960s. The report to the 1961 General Convention begins on what can only be considered a down note: "Both churches consider that the door is open" and then goes on to state that "we are bound to report that no substantial progress has been made in the past three years." The report identifies three major stumbling blocks.

One is "the majority of clergy and laity in the two churches are not yet convinced that union is an urgent issue. We deplore this apathy." It's important to highlight the emphasis on "unity," which is addressed in the second stumbling block. The two churches had been proceeding on a two-fold path: first "intercommunion," with ministers of each church able to celebrate in one another's churches, followed by "organic or corporate union." The proposal was for eventual merger between the Methodist Church and the Episcopal Church, so to create a single entity. This was the Episcopal Church's stated ecumenical policy and goal during this period, as evidenced by a similar proposal in 1943 for organic union with the United Presbyterian Church.

The third point addresses a particular aspect of Methodist and Anglican relations: while Methodists and Episcopalians have much in common, including shared past in Anglicanism, and while there are no major church-dividing theological issues, nonetheless the two churches have developed distinctive emphases. The 1961 report notes that while Methodists and Episcopalians "have much in common and their official formularies are very similar, there are deep and subtle differences in their practical methods and points of view." Episcopalians, for instance, seemed surprised to find that "there is less requirement of uniformity to the official standards of faith and worship" in the Methodist Church than in the Episcopal Church. The report concludes by stating there needs to be more sustained efforts to work together "in certain common

---

7 *Journal of the General Convention of the Protestant Episcopal Church in the United States of America* (1958), Report of the Joint Commission on Approaches to Unity, 715.

tasks, such as Christian education and social relations," and "there must be more acquaintance on local, regional, and national levels" between the two churches.[8]

Reading the reports from the dialogue from 1953 to 1961, one almost gets the impression that it is a kind of repeat of the overtures between White and Coke. The dialogue was a limited one—in this case, not between individuals as with White and Coke, but nonetheless between small groups of bishops and scholars, and once a formal proposal was put on the table, some of the differences in ethos revealed themselves. There also seems to have been little effort to bring together Methodists and Episcopalians on the local or regional levels, or to engage in common mission and ministry. Such efforts are mentioned nowhere in the 1955 or 1958 reports, and the third (and final) report in 1961 ends by stressing the need for cooperation at the local and regional levels as critical to any future discussions.

With the official dialogue having reached a kind of impasse, it is fortunate that a game-changing event emerged to prevent Methodists and Episcopalians from retreating from dialogue with one another for another century. In 1960, Eugene Carson Blake, Stated Clerk of the United Presbyterian Church, preached a sermon at Grace Cathedral of the Episcopal Diocese of California, calling for a church "truly catholic and truly reformed." The first churches to meet to discuss this proposal included the United Presbyterian Church, the Episcopal Church, and the Methodist Church. It was through the participation of the Methodist Church that this call was amended to be a church "truly evangelical, truly catholic, and truly reformed."[9] Nine American churches would eventually join what would be called the Consultation on Church Union (COCU). The impact of COCU's formation on dialogues between the Methodist Church and the Episcopal Church was significant. The conversations from the 1950s, already at an impasse, were rolled into the Consultation on Church Union, and for over thirty years there were no bilateral dialogues between the Methodist Church (which became the United Methodist Church in 1968 following merger with the United Evangelical Brethren) and the Episcopal Church.[10]

---

8 *Journal of the General Convention of the Protestant Episcopal Church in the United States of America* (1961), Report of the Joint Commission on Approaches to Unity, 740–742.

9 For the history of the Episcopal Church's participation in the formation of COCU, see *Journal of the General Convention of the Protestant Episcopal Church in the United States of America* (1964), Report of the Joint Commission on Approaches to Unity, 951–959.

10 For a brief history of COCU, see Paul Crow, "From COCU to CUiC: the Struggle for Reconciliation and Faithfulness," *Journal of Presbyterian History* (84:2), 123–138.

Anglican-Methodist Dialogues in the UK and International Dialogues

This is not to say that there were not other dialogues between Anglicans and Methodists in the postwar period. In particular, Anglicans and Methodists in the United Kingdom have engaged in several rounds of dialogue. Archbishop of Canterbury Geoffrey Fisher preached a sermon in 1946 that invited non-episcopal churches into conversation, resulting in a significant dialogue with the Methodist Church. Reunion proposals were presented to both churches and were approved by the Methodist Church, only to fail narrowly in 1972 to reach the required three-fourths supermajority (though surpassing seventy percent in favor) in the Church of England. A second round of dialogue, which included the Moravian Church and the United Reformed Church in addition to the Methodist Church, also resulted in a proposal that failed to pass in the General Synod of the Church of England in 1982. In 1994, the Methodist Church reached out to invite the Church of England to engage in another round of dialogue.[11]

There would also be an important international dialogue, sponsored by the Anglican Communion and the World Methodist Council, which issued its report, "Sharing in the Apostolic Communion," in 1996. While noting differences between Methodists and Anglicans on episcopacy and ordering of ministry, it also noted substantive agreement in many doctrinal areas, specifically noting that Anglicans and Methodists shared "core doctrine" of the Christian faith, and that Anglicans required "no further doctrinal assurances" from Methodists.[12] "Sharing in the Apostolic Communion" was presented to the Lambeth Conference of 1998, which commended it to provinces of the Communion for further conversation, and encouraged formation of dialogues with Methodists throughout the Anglican Communion.

As a result of the work of the international dialogue, and the overture from the Methodist Church, bilateral dialogues between Methodists and Anglicans in the UK were renewed in the 1990s and 2000s. The Church of England and the British Methodist Church began a new round of dialogue, resulting in the Anglican-Methodist Covenant of 2002, signed by Queen Elizabeth II and the president of the Methodist

---

11 For a discussion of Anglican-Methodist dialogues in the UK, see *An Anglican Methodist Covenant* (London: Methodist Publishing House and Church House Publishing, 2001), 54–67.

12 See "Sharing in the Apostolic Communion," 15–17 . Available online at http://www. anglicancommunion.org/ministry/ecumenical/dialogues/methodist/docs/apostolic_ communion1996.cfm.

Conference. The Covenant committed Anglicans and Methodists to continued dialogue on questions of episcopacy and sharing in ordained ministry, while pledging cooperation in many areas of shared mission and ministry. Conversation continues, as Anglicans and Methodists in the UK ponder how to share in the historic episcopate as part of a commitment to the full, visible unity of the church. A Joint Implementation Committee was formed, which has issued regular updates on the continued dialogues.

A Renewed Dialogue between the Episcopal Church and the United Methodist Church

In the United States, the commending of the work of the international dialogue by the 1998 Lambeth Conference helped to begin a process of renewed dialogue. Perhaps more important, however, was the situation within the Consultation on Church Union. COCU presented several plans for deeper unity, from a proposal for organic merger in its "Plan of Union" in 1970 to a process of covenanting in 1989. None of COCU's proposals, however, were able to garner approval by all of the member communions. At its plenary in 1999, COCU considered a number of possible ways forward. The most significant was the commitment of churches to overcoming the sin of racism, resulting in the re-formation in 2002 of COCU as Churches Uniting in Christ (CUIC). In addition, the plenary acknowledged relationships between churches within COCU (such as dialogues between the historically African American Methodist churches) and between member churches and non-COCU members (such as the Episcopal Church and the Evangelical Lutheran Church in America).[13] Emerging from the plenary was the sense that perhaps progress might be made in bilateral dialogues, as opposed to multilateral conversations, especially since some churches had specific issues and concerns not shared by others. Most likely the plenary had in mind the Presbyterian Church, USA, and the Episcopal Church, the two churches that had historically voiced the greatest concerns around some of COCU's proposals regarding polity, liturgy, and ministry. Previously, bilateral dialogues between members had been discouraged in favor of the multilateral forum of COCU. The Presbyterian Church, USA, and the Episcopal Church both approved the beginning of a bilateral dialogue in 2000. Accordingly, leadership of the United

---

13 See the "Consultation on Church Union: Proceedings of the Eighteenth Plenary," *Mid-Stream* (39:1–2), 1–141.

Methodist Church and the Episcopal Church also believed that progress could be made in a bilateral dialogue. In 2000, the General Conference of the United Methodist Church and the General Convention of the Episcopal Church both approved the beginning of a bilateral dialogue.

The bilateral dialogue met from 2002 to 2010, and unfolded in several stages. Though approved initially by the United Methodist Church and the Episcopal Church, from 2000 to 2002 invitations were circulated to leadership of the historically African American Methodist churches—the African Methodist Episcopal Church (AME), the African Methodist Episcopal Church Zion (AMEZ), and the Christian Methodist Episcopal Church (CME), all of whom have been constituent members of COCU. The AME, CME, and AMEZ, however, were engaged in substantive dialogue with the United Methodist Church in the context of the Pan Methodist Commission, and did not enter in the dialogue with the Episcopal Church so as to concentrate on those efforts, which resulted in a common declaration of full communion in 2008 between the United Methodist Church and the AME, AMEZ, and CME, as well as two other historically African American Methodist bodies, the African Union Methodist Protestant Church (AUMP) and the Union American Methodist Episcopal Church (UAME).

From 2002 to 2006, the bilateral dialogue focused on core aspects of Christian doctrine, and drafted a resolution to propose a relationship of Interim Eucharistic Sharing. In Interim Eucharistic Sharing, communions declare that their core teachings are compatible with the historic Christian faith, and agree to share in joint worship, under certain guidelines and provisions, while at the same time committing to continued dialogue on areas where there is not convergence. The Council of Bishops of the United Methodist Church approved a resolution for Interim Eucharistic Sharing in 2005, which was affirmed by the General Conference of 2008. The 2006 General Convention of the Episcopal Church passed an identical resolution.[14]

From 2006 to 2010, following the establishment of Interim Eucharistic Sharing, the dialogue team continued to meet and to examine the remaining issues dividing the two churches. In 2010, this round of dialogue was completed, and "A Theological Foundation for Full Communion" was issued. In this document, the work of the dialogue from 2002 to 2010 is summarized and key areas of convergence and divergence are noted. The dialogue proposed that both churches

---

14 See Resolution A055 from the 2006 General Convention and Resolution 81456-IC-NonDis of the 2008 United Methodist General Conference.

consider moving forward with a proposal for full communion, including interchangeability of ordained ministries and sharing in the historic episcopate. In 2011, a process towards drafting a proposal of full communion was begun.

Throughout the course of the bilateral dialogue, particular attention was paid to the issues of race and racism and in outreach to the historically African American Methodist Churches. A consultation was held in 2006 at the Interdenominational Theological Center in Atlanta, Georgia, involving African American representatives from the United Methodist Church as well as from the AME, CME, and AMEZ. In 2008 and 2009, consultations were held involving bishops, scholars, and clergy from the UMC, AME, AMEZ, CME, and the Episcopal Church, examining the histories of race and racism in and among the participants. The dialogue team continues to be in dialogue with the AME, AMEZ, and CME, to see how the Episcopal Church might be brought into deeper ecclesial partnership with these historic aspects of American Methodism.

The dialogue has also been in regular consultation with broader Anglican and Methodist dialogues. In 2007 a consultation was held in London with representatives from the dialogue between the Church of England and the British Methodist Church. Also in 2007 the World Methodist Council and Anglican Communion established the Anglican Methodist International Consultation on Unity and Mission (AMICUM), whose charge was to examine the current state of Anglican-Methodist relations throughout both communions. In 2012, AMICUM met in the United States and included participation from the Episcopal Church and the United Methodist Church.

Conclusion

Other essays in this collection will focus on important theological, liturgical, ecclesiological, and ethical questions concerning the proposal for full communion between the Episcopal Church and the United Methodist Church. In looking at the history of dialogue between the two communions, it is important to keep in mind several aspects of our past histories as we look forward:

- Every dialogue between Anglicans and Methodists has stated there are no substantive, church-dividing theological issues between Anglicans and Methodists. This does not mean there is complete unity of thought, but that there is nothing on the order of, say, believers' baptism or papal infallibility.

- There have, however, been significant divisions in terms of race and class. These are matters that the modern ecumenical movement has not spent much of its first century addressing, focusing instead on matters of ordained ministry, sacramental theology, and ecclesiology. Episcopalians and United Methodists have the potential to make an important contribution to the ecumenical movement in addressing these matters, which some might argue are the true church dividing issues in American religion.

- The past century has seen movements towards commonality and convergence between Episcopalians and United Methodists. Can we see this coming together as looking forward as much as looking back? What potential exists if we can continue to be changed and transformed as we move forward along these trajectories of convergence and commonality?

- We must be cautious not to repeat the same mistakes as the dialogue from the 1950s. Can we overcome a lack of urgency from clergy and laity that United Methodists and Episcopalians should be striving for deeper unity in mission and ministry? Can we address differences in ethos as well as dealing with theological and ecclesiological questions? Can we engage the churches on the local and regional levels? The dialogue in the 1950s did not address those questions soon enough or consistently enough.

- One element which is perhaps more important in our current reality than in our past histories is the impact of globalization on both of our churches. The Episcopal Church has congregations in more than sixteen countries, and the Central Conferences (overseas jurisdictions of the United Methodist Church) made up nearly 40 percent of delegates to the 2012 General Conference. How do we translate the historical reality birthed in the context of the United States into what have become global churches?

While United Methodists and Episcopalians may have been caught in a parent trap, living separate ecclesial lives, in the past decades we have seen enormous progress in dialogues here in the United States, the United Kingdom, and globally. Perhaps God is calling us at this movement to the difficult work of healing the sins of separation inherited from our forebears.

Thomas Ferguson is Dean of Bexley Hall Seminary in Columbus, Ohio. He served as Associate Deputy to the Presiding Bishop for Ecumenical and Interreligious Relations, and as Deputy to the Presiding Bishop for Ecumenical and Interreligious Relations. He also served as staff support to the Episcopal Church-United Methodist Church Dialogue Team.

CHAPTER 3

A Review of Sacramental and Liturgical Matters

Patrick Malloy

Questions of "sacramental efficacy" were at the heart of the sixteenth-century reformation. Theologians asked if God actually does something to human beings and material objects when the sacraments are celebrated or if human beings merely remind themselves during those rituals of something God has already done. The debate occupied Anglican, continental Protestant, and Roman Catholic reformers.

The Church of England—a "parent" of both the Episcopal Church and the United Methodist Church—was shaped and informed by a number of notable theologians. Yet, it gives none of them or their writings the singular status that, say, Presbyterians give John Calvin and his *Institutes*. In fact, under the leadership of Elizabeth I, the Church of England sought a way for Anglicans to subscribe to the views of a number of theologians and yet remain within the embrace of the church. This embrace, outlined by the Articles of Religion, the early creeds, the First Seven Councils of the Undivided Church, the Book of Common Prayer, and, of course, the scriptures, was generous. Anglicans aimed for shared conviction about core things and openness about secondary things.

Because of this, Anglicans enter ecumenical dialogues with a challenge that members of many other Christian traditions do not. Unlike Roman Catholics (who can rely upon the statements of their hierarchy) or Lutherans (who have recourse to the writings of Martin Luther), Episcopalians have a far less definitive body of texts or traditions upon which to base their positions.

Methodists find themselves in a position very much like Anglicans. John Wesley, the founder of the Methodist movement and a priest

31

in the Church of England, is a singular figure in the history of the
United Methodist Church, who brought with him an Anglican sensibility. Since its founding days, however, Methodism has confronted
a great many historical realities that have taken the church far from
John Wesley and his brand of Anglicanism. "During the nineteenth and
twentieth centuries," for example, "the rich Wesleyan understandings of
the Eucharist were lost."[1] The merger of the Methodist Church in 1968
with the Evangelical United Brethren surely enriched the church, but
also drew it further from its Anglican and Wesleyan roots. A dialogue
between the United Methodist Church and the Episcopal Church, then,
is not really a dialogue—a one-to-one interchange—but a conversation
with many voices on both sides. Since neither church is of one mind on
many things, a simple dialogue is impossible.

The United Methodist Church has produced official "white papers"
on Baptism and the Holy Eucharist.[2] The Episcopal Church has not. At
first glance, this makes dialogue with the United Methodists on these
issues simpler than dialogue with Episcopalians. These documents,
however, do not have the binding force on Methodists that the Book of
Common Prayer has on Episcopalians. Once again, then, the dynamic
of this important conversation between children of the same parent is
not as simple as the word "dialogue" would suggest.

In 2010, the Episcopal–United Methodist Dialogue Team issued a
document preparing for a full communion agreement, but most of the
document is not about agreement. Most of the document deals with
"Issues Perceived as Separating Our Churches." Four of those issues
are explicitly liturgical or sacramental, and in each case, the issues are
complex.

The Relationship between Baptism and Salvation

Episcopalians claim to have been "born again" in Baptism, usually as infants. Being born again does not require any experience or
decision on the part of the infant but is an entirely free gift of God.
"Historic Christian teaching—including that of Eastern Orthodox,
Roman Catholic, and Lutheran Churches—maintained that Baptism is
the divinely appointed means through which human beings are born

---

1 "This Holy Mystery: A United Methodist Understanding of Holy Communion," 6.
2 "This Holy Mystery" and "By Water and the Spirit: A United Methodist Understanding of
  Baptism."

again in Christ and through which their sins are forgiven."[3] This is called "regeneration": a moral change making a person justified and disposed toward the Christian life. Every Episcopal edition of the Book of Common Prayer including the current one claims this. The 1979 Prayer Book says explicitly that Baptism confers "the forgiveness of sin," "the life of grace," and the seal of the Holy Spirit. It marks a person "as Christ's own forever."[4] This is being "born again." All the editions of the Episcopal Prayer Book before the current one asserted in a post-baptismal bidding that "this child is regenerate, and grafted into the Body of Christ's Church."

John Wesley, in adopting the 1662 English Book of Common Prayer (which contained this same bidding) for North American Methodists excised the word "regenerate," saying only "*this Child* is grafted into the body of Christ's Church."[5] Methodist liturgical scholar James White noted that, while Wesley omitted the word "regenerate" in that one post-baptismal text, he did retain it in a collect preceding the water-bath.[6] In other writings, Wesley claimed that Baptism is regenerative, but he recognized that through sin and a failure to make a personal commitment to Christ, the grace given in the sacrament can be "rendered ineffective."[7]

When he wrote of regeneration, Wesley often did not mention Baptism, but that does not mean that he denied that God confers regeneration in Baptism. If I were to write about the human capacity to think, for example, I probably would not mention breathing, because I would take for granted that thinking human beings breathe. Similarly, Wesley, in his historic and cultural context, when he wrote about regeneration could take for granted that everyone in his orbit had been baptized in infancy.

Just as the nineteenth century saw the erosion of Wesley's eucharistic theology, so "from the nineteenth century, Methodist interpreters of Christian theology laid great emphasis on the conversion experience, not as a necessary development of regeneration, but as the normal means

---

3 "A Theological Foundation for Full Communion between The Episcopal Church and The United Methodist Church," 18.

4 The Book of Common Prayer (New York: Church Hymnal, 1979), 308.

5 John Wesley, *The Sunday Service of the Methodists in North America with Other Occasional Services* in *John Wesley's Sunday Service of the Methodists in North America with an Introduction by James White* (Nashville: Quarterly Review, 1984), 142.

6 James White, introduction to *The Sunday Service of the Methodists in North America with Other Occasional Services,* by John Wesley (Nashville: Quarterly Review, 1984), 29.

7 "By Water and the Spirit," 1.

of regeneration."[8] They tended to see Baptism only as a marker that a person was being incorporated into the Christian community. That incorporation did not automatically mean that the person was being "born again" or ever would be "born again." Baptism, in this view, prepares a person to be reborn by making her a part of a community of faith, repentance, and good works, but Baptism itself does not effect rebirth. Hearkening back to the reformation debate about whether the sacraments are effective, nineteenth-century Methodists came to see Baptism not as "an act of divine grace" but "an expression of human choice."[9]

The introduction to the baptismal rite in the current United Methodist Book of Worship is clear about this.

> While Baptism signifies the whole working of God's grace, much that it signifies, from the washing away of sin to the pouring out of the Holy Spirit, will need to happen during the course of a lifetime. If an act of personal Christian commitment has taken place, Baptism celebrates that act and the grace of God that made it possible. If such an act has not yet taken place, Baptism anticipates that act, declares its necessity, and celebrates God's grace that will make it possible.[10]

Baptism, according to the United Methodist Book of Worship, either celebrates the rebirth of those who have already had an experience of conversion or brings into the church those too young to have been converted, setting them on a path toward being "born again" through nurture and formation. In either case, Baptism does not effect "rebirth," that is, "regeneration."

To be clear, this statement in the current Methodist liturgical book does not imply that God is not active in Baptism. All good and right actions come from God through prevenient grace, that is, the grace that comes before and leads to every good work. God's prevenient grace leads a child's guardians to bring the child to the font. God's prevenient grace beckons the baptized child toward conversion and moral regeneration. This, however, does not mean that what happens in Baptism *is* moral regeneration. Although the United Methodist Baptismal rite itself

---

8 "A Theological Foundation," 19.
9 "By Water and the Spirit," 2.
10 *The United Methodist Book of Worship* (Nashville: The United Methodist Publishing House, 1992), 82.

seems in a number of places to suggest that Baptism is regenerative, the framers of the rite deny that they intended to make such a claim.[11]

For Episcopalians, "baptismal regeneration" is a matter of historical as well as theological significance. In 1873, a small but influential number of Episcopalians concluded that the Prayer Book liturgy contained "germs" of what they derisively called "Romish" beliefs. This led them to secede and form the Reformed Episcopal Church—the first group ever to break away from the Episcopal Church. That body still exists.[12] Chief among their complaints was that the Prayer Book claims that Baptism bestows regeneration, a claim they entirely rejected.[13] As the United Methodist-Episcopal dialogue team has written, however, this claim is not "Romish" at all but is the claim of Christianity across time and place. Still, history has moved the United Methodist Church to agree with the Reformed Episcopal Church and has led it into to a different vision of how a Christian comes to be born again.

"Baptismal regeneration," then, is an area of disagreement between United Methodists and Episcopalians. The two churches agree that God establishes a covenant in Baptism that cannot be destroyed by sin. God is faithful to the covenant even when baptized Christians are not. "The bond which God establishes in Baptism is indissoluble,"[14] the Book of Common Prayer asserts. The United Methodist Church agrees that the baptismal bond is indissoluble, but it does not understand the bond as "regeneration" or "rebirth."

While they are consistent with the ancient and generally accepted Christian viewpoint in claiming that God confers regeneration in Baptism, in this Episcopalians set the stage for great misunderstandings. Many nominal Episcopalians, who have neither a relationship to the community of faith nor an intentional religious practice, rush their children to Baptism, presumably to assure their eternal salvation. This is based on an assumption, entirely incorrect, that the Episcopal Church teaches that God will not save those who are not baptized. While Baptism is the "divinely appointed" means by which regeneration occurs, it is not the *only* means. There are an infinite number of ways by which the infinite God can choose to be reconciled to human beings. God can, if God chooses, save those who are not baptized.

---

11 "A Theological Foundation," 20.

12 http://rechurch.org

13 Allen C. Guelzo, *For the Union of Evangelical Christendom: The Irony of the Reformed Episcopalians* (University Park: Pennsylvania State University Press, 1994), 65–66, 109–110.

14 BCP, 298.

For our two churches to move forward, the notion of "regeneration" must be carefully defined. What exactly do United Methodists deny happening in Baptism that Episcopalians insist does happen?[15] How much is it a matter of conviction, and how much is it a matter of vocabulary? The United Methodist Church affirms that God, in the waters of Baptism, enters into a permanent covenant with the baptized. Since the covenant is irrevocable, no baptized people—no matter the church in which they were baptized—should or may ever be baptized again. To do so would suggest that God is not forever faithful to God's covenant. The Episcopal Church agrees, and further agrees that God is forever faithful to the covenant even if human beings are not. There is a great deal of agreement here. The sticking point is not whether God acts in Baptism but what exactly that action is.

The Eucharist: The Presence of Christ

Among the eucharistic texts in the Episcopal Hymnal 1982, few express so clear a belief in the real presence of Christ in the Holy Communion as the texts by John and Charles Wesley. Wesleyan eucharistic theology was entirely consistent with the theology of the Church of England. In fact, John Wesley is often thought to have more strongly affirmed and more strongly valued the eucharistic real presence than many of his Anglican contemporaries.

With only one significant exception, reformation theologians accepted as a matter of course that the church comes to know the presence of Christ in the Eucharist because, as the church from its earliest days expressed it, God the Father through the action of the Holy Spirit makes Christ himself present. How this happens, not whether it happens, was the question. Only the Swiss reformer, Ulrich Zwingli, denied it, claiming that the Eucharist is only a memorial of Jesus' saving acts and an inspiration for deeper faith and Christian community. The issue for Zwingli was one of simple distance. It is impossible for an embodied human person to be in multiple places at once, he reasoned, and since Jesus is (reading the story of the Ascension literally) in a place called heaven, how can he be in the Holy Communion?

As the other reformers worked to find a way to articulate how Jesus could be present in both the Eucharist and in heaven, they all agreed on one thing. The medieval doctrine of transubstantiation was not a useful

---

15 The issue of Arminianism, a theology that United Methodists embrace and Anglicans have been accused of (but deny) embracing, must be part of this discussion.

way to talk about the mystery. The Methodist Articles of Religion borrow the explicit renunciation of transubstantiation from the Anglican Articles. Yet, as the document "This Holy Mystery" admits, that renunciation can only be understood as part of a complex and often vicious battle against the Roman Catholic Church.[16]

"Transubstantiation" is a widely misunderstood term. Most medieval Christians clung to it, but few except the theologians understood it. Theologians were using Aristotle's way of understanding created reality to describe how Jesus can be both ascended into glory and present in the Holy Communion. They claimed that, in the Eucharist, the "substance" of bread and wine are transformed into the "substance" of Christ. "Substance," in common speech, means the physical nature of a thing. Aristotle used the word, however, in precisely the opposite way. For him, "substance" is the non-physical aspect of a thing, which makes it what it is. It has none of the characteristics of physical nature: shape, for example, weight, color, or even locale. The doctrine of transubstantiation, then, actually teaches that Jesus is *not* physically present in the Eucharist but is present in a real, non-physical way. What one receives when one receives Communion is in every physical sense bread and wine. Yet, its ultimate reality is something else: the presence of Christ.

It is useful, by way of analogy, to think of the "substance" of a thing like the "soul" of a person. What people think of as a soul has no physical characteristics. It has no weight, no color or shape, no smell or taste. It does not exist in a place. (Where, for example, if you believe in the human soul, does it reside in the body? Is it in the hand? In the foot? In the brain? In the heart?) Transubstantiation, then, explicitly denies that Christ is physically present in the Eucharist, but affirms that he is *really* present.

In rejecting this Aristotelian way of describing the mystery of Christ's real presence, the reformers were forced to devise other ways to explain how Jesus could be both in heaven and in actual contact with those who partake of Holy Communion. The Book of Common Prayer and the other formulations of the Church of England, which Wesley would have accepted, do not set forth a particular way of speaking of this mystery. The theologian Richard Hooker articulated what is often considered the standard Anglican approach by focusing not on what happens to the bread and wine, but what happens to believers as they receive the bread and wine. Hooker said that transubstantiation is an apt word for describing the eucharistic change, but he suggested that

---

16 "This Holy Mystery," 32.

what is transubstantiated is the person receiving the sacrament, not the bread and wine.[17] When the food and drink are set aside by the church through prayer, they become a means by which Jesus offers himself to communicants and becomes truly present to those who receive the sacrament in faith. This is not the only way an Episcopalian might understand the real presence, but it is certainly a standard Anglican approach. It seems to be entirely consistent with the statement of the United Methodist Church concerning the real presence.

> For United Methodists, the Lord's Supper is anchored in the life of the historical Jesus of Nazareth, but is not primarily a remembrance or memorial. We do not embrace the medieval doctrine of transubstantiation, though we do believe that the elements are essential tangible means through which God works. We understand the presence in temporal and relational terms.[18]

In other words: In the Eucharist Jesus is present now (temporal) so he can meet (relational) those who desire him. This happens precisely through the bread and wine (tangible means) because God makes it so (God works). It is hard to see why, then, the issue of Jesus' real presence in the Eucharist is a matter of dispute. The only question is whether the position articulated in the United Methodist "white paper" is, in fact, a position that many Methodists would espouse, and whether what is embedded in the Book of Common Prayer is what Episcopalians actually believe.

Both the Episcopal Church and the United Methodist Church agree, too, that the elements, once consecrated, must never again be treated as ordinary food and drink. They must be consumed or, according to the discipline of the United Methodist Church, returned to the earth through burial or scattering. The intention, however, is the same. Once God takes these things as instruments by which Christ is really made present, they are sacred.

The problem seems not to be a conflict in official statements but in actual belief. In the nineteenth century, the eucharistic theology of Methodists (and most other American Protestants) and the eucharistic theology of Episcopalians (and most other Anglicans) drifted in

---

17 Richard Hooker, *Of the Laws of Ecclesiastical Piety* (1593), V.57.11. http://oll.libertyfund. org/?option=com_staticxt&staticfile=show.php%3Ftitle=922&chapter=85486&layout=htm l&Itemid=27 accessed 7 August 2013.
18 "The Holy Mystery," 13.

opposite directions. Methodists, in response to frontier revivalism, drifted in a Zwinglian direction. Episcopalians, in response to the theological Oxford Movement and the architectural and ritual Cambridge Movement, moved in a more patristic or medieval direction. Neither church, however, officially changed its position, as expressed in its liturgy, about the eucharistic real presence.

Episcopalians today, while insisting that Christ is really present in the Eucharist, must honor the wide range of ways this mystery is understood among them. Methodists, while defending their tradition's abandonment of the medieval concept, "transubstantiation," must honor Wesley's belief in the real presence, recognizing, moreover, that in Article XVIII he was defending the ancient and universal belief of all Christians over against the Zwinglian view. With these commitments in place, United Methodists and Episcopalians can surely find an authentic basis for full communion in the mystery of the Eucharist.

The Eucharist: The Meal of the Baptized

At its 2012 General Convention, the Episcopal Church reaffirmed that, according to ancient custom, Holy Communion is administered *normatively* only to the baptized. "The Wesleyan tradition has always recognized that Holy Communion may be an occasion for the reception of converting, justifying, and sanctifying grace" by the unbaptized.[19] On the surface, these two positions contradict one another.

The 2012 affirmation of the Episcopal Church was simple and direct.

> The Episcopal Church reaffirms that Baptism is the ancient and normative entry point to receiving Holy Communion and that our Lord Jesus Christ calls us to go into the world and baptize all peoples.[20]

This resolution is noteworthy because another one was rejected that proposed eliminating the requirement of Baptism before Holy Communion from the Prayer Book and the Canons.[21]

Note, however, that the resolution that *did* pass does not deny that unbaptized people who receive Holy Communion can be converted by the experience. Many people have come to conversion and have been led to Baptism by receiving the eucharistic sacrament. This, however, in

---

19 "By Water and Spirit," 13.
20 Resolution C029.
21 Resolution C040.

the view of the Episcopal Church, is not *normative*. The word "norma-tive" does not mean "normal" or "usual." It means "standard-setting." So while unbaptized people may, indeed, be converted by receiving Holy Communion, the Episcopal Church considers this to be excep-tional and outside the way the church, when it is living out its self-understanding, operates.

What is the normative standard, then, is a key question. The United Methodist Church is not clear. Its official statement on Baptism does say, "Unbaptized persons who receive Holy Communion should be coun-seled and nurtured toward Baptism as soon as possible," suggesting that Holy Communion without Baptism is not normative for that church either. It is not discouraged, but it is not normative. The sharing in Holy Communion by the unbaptized should trigger the enactment of the *normative* pattern. Holy Communion and Baptism are integrally connected.[22]

The difference in understandings of how Baptism relates to Holy Communion also points to the nineteenth-century drift of the two churches in opposite ecclesiological directions. The Methodist Church, under the influence of frontier revivalism, placed an increasingly greater emphasis on the conversion of the individual, while the Episcopal Church, under the influence of the Oxford Movement, placed an increasingly greater emphasis on the church, constituted according to historic patterns. These tendencies are called, respectively, "low church" and "high church," based upon the place they give the institution in the dynamic of salvation. Naturally, then, United Methodists today would value the conversion of the individual over the normative practice of the church, while the Episcopal Church would see the normative practice of the church as the vehicle by which the individual is converted. This "high church" tendency is why the practice of the Christian church across time and space is important to Episcopalians. They cling to the tradition of inviting only the baptized to Holy Communion because it is attested to as early as 150 CE by Justin Martyr and eventually—if not by that time—became "the broad consensus of Christian tradition and practice."[23]

The difference in how the two churches view the relationship between Baptism and Eucharist is also, no doubt, tied to the two churches' dif-fering views of how regeneration occurs. The Episcopal Church claims that rebirth, that is, regeneration, is given in Baptism and logically pre-cedes receiving the eucharistic Body of Christ. (Christians are made

---

22 "By Water and the Spirit," 13.
23 "A Theological Foundation," 25.

members of the Body of Christ by Baptism. They take into themselves, therefore, the eucharistic Body of Christ to become what we already are, offering "ourselves, our souls, and bodies," with Christ.) United Methodists, however, place a higher value on personal conversion as the occasion of regeneration, and this conversion may be fostered or triggered by the reception of Holy Communion. (Taken by Christ into his Body through receiving the eucharistic sacrament, which is a conversion experience, they symbol-forth this new reality through the sacrament of Baptism.) These two approaches seem to be quite divergent, but, clearly, there is more agreement here than at first meets the eye.

Still, agreement or not, there is danger, at least for Episcopalians, should the United Methodist Church and the Episcopal Church enter into full communion. The Episcopal Church is in the midst of theological and pastoral reflection on the issue of "opening the table" to the unbaptized. One of the greatest gains in the liturgical renewal that took shape in the 1979 Book of Common Prayer is what Episcopalians commonly call a "baptismal ecclesiology." This means that the Church is constituted by Baptism, not Holy Orders, and that all the baptized are ministers of this church. That makes Baptism foundational. When Baptism is abandoned as the portal into the life of the church, the logic of the 1979 Prayer Book is undermined. This is not to suggest that God's grace is restricted to the sacramental structures of the church. It is only to suggest that a decision to reject the *norm* that Baptism is the ordinary way by which people are made regenerate and, therefore, part of the community of the saints, would be a significant decision. Such a significant change in Episcopal theology and practice cannot be tripped into. Full communion agreements are clear that they do not create one church out of two. If the United Methodist Church and the Episcopal Church were to decide to enter into full communion, neither church should automatically assume the sacramental discipline of the other. Entering into full communion with the United Methodists cannot be a "backdoor" method for radically shifting the assumptions of the Episcopal Church about ecclesiology, soteriology (how people are saved), or sacramental theology.

The Elements of the Eucharist

The eucharistic institution narratives in the Synoptic Gospels and 1 Corinthians recount Jesus, according to Jewish custom, attaching symbolic meaning to bread and wine. The Episcopal Church uses these elements in celebrating Holy Communion, while the United Methodist

Church, "in the wake of the temperance movement and Methodists' adoption of the ideal of total abstinence from beverage alcohol,"[24] uses unfermented grape juice instead of wine.

This is not the first time Anglicans have had to wrestle with the question of what is suitable food and drink for the Lord's Supper. In 2001, the International Anglican Liturgical Consultation, meeting in Berkeley, California, heard reports from across the Anglican Communion about the use of other elements.[25] Substitutions have been made (in some cases, imposed by the hierarchy) for both bread and wine because of local prohibitions against the use of alcohol for any purpose, the impossibility of securing wheat bread or grape wine, or a conviction that the appropriate elements are the cultural equivalents of wheat bread and grape wine rather than those specific elements. Already in many Episcopal congregations, grape juice is consecrated along with wine to make it possible for people with alcoholism to receive Holy Communion under both forms.

This practice, not accounted for in the Prayer Book's rubrics, points to an issue that is important within the Episcopal Church and in the dialogue with United Methodists. The Book of Common Prayer mandates that the altar should be prepared for the Eucharistic Prayer with only one chalice, underscoring that "the one bread and one cup" are symbols of the unified Body of Christ, the Church. Additional wine, necessary for communing the assembly, is to be placed on the Lord's Table in flagons that can be poured, after the Eucharistic Prayer, into auxiliary chalices. Already, Episcopalians are violating this rubric, although hardly universally, by having two chalices on the Holy Table during the Eucharistic Prayer: one with wine and one with grape juice. United Methodists sometimes use trays of small communion cups rather than a single chalice with flagons, a practice also at odds with the rubrics and intention of the Book of Common Prayer: one Bread and one Cup, one Body and one Lord.

The Methodist-Episcopal dialogue team has proposed the adoption of the Book of Common Prayer approach but with separate flagons for alcoholic wine and for wine without alcohol. It has recommended the use of a single chalice and, in place of grape juice, de-alcoholized wine. This compromise ensures that alcoholic and non-alcoholic wine are always consecrated, safeguarding the sensibilities of both Episcopalians and Methodists, and safeguarding as well the symbolism of the single

---

24 "A Theological Foundation," 24.
25 http://www.anglicancommunion.org/resources/liturgy/docs/ialc2001minutes. cfm, accessed 8 August 2013.

elements divided and shared. There would be but one cup on the Holy Table during the Eucharistic Prayer even if the flagons were to contain two kinds of wine.

Similarly, the team proposes that whatever of the sacrament remains after the liturgy be disposed of reverently. This is already the custom of both churches, although the Book of Common Prayer insists that this be by eating and drinking, while the United Methodist Church's Book of Worship allows for returning the bread and wine to the earth.[26] (The 1662 English Book of Common Prayer upon which Wesley based his Sunday service also insisted that the unused elements be consumed. This directive, along with many others appended to the 1662 Communion service, was not included in Wesley's *Sunday Service of the Methodists in North America*. Because all of the directives were omitted, Wesley's intention about this one rubric cannot be ascertained.)

What is called for in both churches if the proposals of the United Methodist-Episcopal team are put into practice is catechesis. Episcopalians must be introduced to the conversations that have already been carried out in the Anglican Communion about what elements can properly be used for the Lord's Supper. They also must be made aware of the breadth of practice that already exists. United Methodists, on the other hand, must be re-rooted in the Wesleyan eucharistic theology and practice lost in the nineteenth century: lost, it would seem, not as a matter of principle but by accident. The use of actual wine and a single chalice would have been the custom that John Wesley would have known and, it can be assumed, sanctioned.

The Reverend Canon Patrick Malloy, PhD, is Professor of Liturgy in the H. Boone Porter Chair at the General Seminary, New York.

---

26 "This Holy Mystery," 24.

CHAPTER 4

The Beauty of Holiness
and the Holiness of Beauty:
The Delicious and Distinctive Flavors of
United Methodist and Episcopal Worship

Taylor W. Burton-Edwards

A cultural highlight of my most recent trip to Kinshasa, Democratic Republic of the Congo, in 2012 was the opportunity to share a meal with ecumenical colleagues at a Chinese buffet restaurant in the city. The decor and the food selection were typical Chinese, as least by American standards. The servers and cooks were Chinese people making their home in Kinshasa. There were several varieties of rice, Kung Pao chicken, chow mein, lo mein, sushi, sweet and sour pork or chicken, beef with broccoli, wonton soup, and so on. My guess is the recipes, as well, were typical Chinese.

Then I tasted the food. And the flavors were at once delicious and decidedly and unmistakably Congolese.

I'm not a "foodie." I don't have the vocabulary at hand to give a precise description of the differences a culinary expert might. But I might say the food I had eaten in Kinshasa previously, that I have come to identify with that region of Congo, had often been more "earthy," perhaps a bit more "umami" in its overall palate, maybe with a bit more of a "high acid tang" in its hotter spices than what I would typically have associated with cuisines I have sampled in the US, Europe, and Thailand. These three factors together—earthiness, umami, and tang—were noticeable to me in what otherwise appeared to be a typical Chinese restaurant serving a typical Chinese menu. I might almost be tempted to say it was Congolese cuisine with a Chinese veneer, rather than Chinese cuisine with a Congolese twist.

I tell this story because I think it may be a helpful way to describe the similarities and distinct differences in emphasis and flavor, if you will, one might find between worship in the United Methodist Church and in the Episcopal Church, at least in the United States.

Like the Chinese restaurant in Kinshasa, the decor of many United Methodist and Episcopal worship spaces might be very similar to each other. You are likely to find a nave with pews facing forward, the same seasonal colors on banners and paraments, a "divided chancel" that distinguishes where readings and the sermon may take place, and the Lord's Table front and center with room behind it for the pastor or priest to preside while facing the people. There may also be candles and persons specially designated to light them at some point during the opening of worship.

Likewise, the "menu" or order of worship of the two denominations, if you were to place the official ritual of each side by side in outline form, would be nearly identical. United Methodists and Episcopalians share the same "basic pattern" of Entrance, Word, Table, and Sending. We both include a form of the "collect for purity" near the beginning of worship. We both commend the reading of three scriptures and the praying of a Psalm from essentially the same lectionary. We both call for some form of confession of faith in response to the sermon, with prayers following this. We both place the confession of sin, pardon, and the Peace in close proximity to each other. We both note the offering is a time not only for collecting money but also for preparing the Lord's Table. Our Great Thankgivings, while differing in wording, are nearly identical in structure, with an opening dialog, a pre-*Sanctus* anaphora, the *Sanctus/Benedictus*, a post-*Benedictus* anaphora, an account including the *Verba*, a memorial acclamation, an *Epiclesis*, the Lord's Prayer and the fraction. We even both provide music in our hymnals for singing the *Sanctus/Benedictus*, the Memorial Acclamation, the Great Amen, and the *Agnus Dei*.

Yet I daresay, as a United Methodist elder married to an Episcopal priest, despite profound similarities in decor and menu, the flavor of worship we each offer, while delicious in its own right, is also decidedly and unmistakably our own. To United Methodists, Episcopal worship may taste at once more elegant and somewhat less emotionally intense. To Episcopalians, United Methodist worship may taste more emotionally charged, even "driven," while perhaps less elegant or contemplative.

What I'd like to explore is a bit of the history leading us to have these impressions of each other at worship. Then I wish to suggest ways we may find our own flavors of worship and our appreciation for each other's flavor strengthened as we move toward full communion with each other and beyond.

And I'd like to begin by suggesting our unmistakably distinct flavors may have much to do with our differing but equally delicious valuing of beauty and holiness.

Methodism and the Beauty of Holiness

Worship the Lord in the beauty of holiness: come, let us adore him.
—Invitatory to the Psalter for Sundays and Weekdays during Ordinary Time, Book of Common Prayer, 1979, 81

It may seem odd for me to begin a description of the Methodist flavor of our nearly common ritual by quoting from the Book of Common Prayer. Perhaps even more oddly, this line may well be the most commonly used opening of Morning Prayer for Episcopalians throughout the church year. Yet as intrinsic as it is to daily office piety in the Episcopal Church, it also simply and eloquently states what may be the primary driver and goal for the Methodist flavor of worship and Christian life, the "beauty of holiness."

"Holiness" for Methodists is another way of saying what Methodism's founder, Anglican priest John Wesley, also called "perfection in love." It is a life so rooted and centered in love of God and neighbor that it regularly overflows and abounds with acts of goodness, kindness, and gentleness, and with joy in the Lord and all God's creatures. Such "holiness of heart and life" as Wesley and many Methodists have referred to it is, truly, beautiful to behold.

As the Wesleys taught us, holiness is born within us as a gift from God. However, it does not grow in us without our cooperation. The word "our" is critical for Methodists. Wesley was clear as individuals we are incapable of adequately nourishing or sustaining this holiness in ourselves. It takes a small group. More specifically, it takes a small group of persons intending to "flee the wrath to come, and to be saved from sin," a small group in which all members actively watch over one another in love. Wesley is often correctly quoted as saying, "[There is] no religion but social, no holiness but social holiness."[1] Wesley was referring specifically to the need he believed we all have for participation in such accountable small groups if we expect to progress in holiness in our lives.

---

1 John Wesley, from his preface to the 1739 edition of *Hymns and Sacred Poems*.

Indeed, the primary rationale for the organizational design of early Methodism was to make it more likely for more people to experience the beauty of such holiness in their lives, personally and collectively. The typical early Methodist would have attended at least three gatherings, including some form of worship, weekly. On Sunday mornings there was a local congregation, usually an Anglican parish with its ritual defined by the Book of Common Prayer. On Sunday evenings, members of the Methodist societies would attend a society meeting, full of hymn singing, testimony, and exhortatory preaching. These meetings and this form of worship were aimed at encouraging people to continue to strive after holiness in their lives. And on Thursday evenings, Methodists would attend smaller meetings of (ideally) no more than twelve people, sometimes in homes, sometimes in smaller rooms in their society halls, to pray, to gain more instruction, and to report "how it is with their souls," and in so doing challenge and encourage one another toward further holiness of heart and life. Some also participated in what were known as "band societies," even smaller groups, no more than five or so, and always same-sex. Here, persons would "confess their sins to one another that they may be healed." Participation in the band societies was always optional, but participation in a congregation, the society meeting, and a class meeting were mandatory for all seeking to become or remain members in good standing in the Methodist society.

Thus, while most early Methodists were Anglicans, the forms of worship and Christian life they themselves led in their own gatherings (society meetings and class meetings) were much more outwardly emotionally expressive, even, we might say, "driven," corresponding to the Methodist ethos of striving with great zeal after perfection in love in this life.

Much has changed within the wider families of Methodism that now make up the United Methodist Church. Relatively few United Methodists today speak of holiness as the early Methodist leaders (the Wesleys, Francis Asbury, Martin Boehm, Phillip Wilhelm Otterbein, or Jacob Albrecht) did. Today, when United Methodists speak of social holiness, we probably use that term to speak of social justice or making public witness against perceived social injustices. Few of us still use it in its original sense of describing the need for something like a "class meeting" if we expect to grow in holiness of heart and life. By the middle of the nineteenth century, Methodism was by far the most mainstream expression of Christianity in the United States, shedding its earlier sectarian look and feel for a prominent place on Main Street in county seats and larger towns and cities, as well as smaller hamlets, across the continent. At the same time, the structures of the early Methodist Society, with its class meeting and particular ways of worship and devotional practice, faded away. By the time of the creation of the United Methodist Church from the union of the former Evangelical United Brethren and the Methodist Church in 1968, societies and class meetings had been generally absent, or, if vestigially present, in ways nearly unrecognizable from their original forms, for well over a century. By the late nineteenth century, Methodists in general and Methodist worship in particular began to take on a much more intentionally ecumenical form and spirit, a process that has continued and may be especially noticeable in the deep similarities between official United Methodist ritual and the ritual of other Protestants and Roman Catholics who have actively participated with us in global ecumenical movements, institutions, and efforts toward liturgical renewal.

The emphasis on holiness had changed. Structures had changed. Distinctive venues where worship was practiced in distinctive ways were gone. The ritual for Sunday worship had evolved toward an ecumenically recognizable form. But the ethos, and with it, the aesthetics of emotionally expressive, "driven," and exhortatory worship designed to revive the spirit and encourage the heart have continued as an unmistakable hallmark of whatever forms of worship United Methodists have been or are likely to offer. These are the ingredients that mark our distinctive flavor.

Though today United Methodists may rarely speak of holiness of heart and life (certainly in comparison with our EUB and Methodist forebears), I would submit that our worship and our whole way of being Christian is still flavored by an ethos that drives us toward striving and an accompanying aesthetic that values passion, creativity, expressiveness, and exhortation throughout the entire ritual. Evidence of this may be found in vivacious calls to worship, in worship leaders calling the people to sing (or dance!) "like they mean it," in exhortatory pastoral prayers, and even in the way our clergy may preside at the Great Thanksgiving. Consciously or unconsciously, Methodists model nearly all elements of worship as if they were intended to stir the hearts of the people toward God.

This is that delicious, distinctive flavor of United Methodist worship and our way of Christian life. In all things we are expressive, driven, and seek to exhort others. When our worship does that, to us, it is beautiful, because to us, that is what holiness still feels like.

Episcopal Worship: The Holiness of Beauty

> *I believe there is no LITURGY in the World, either in ancient or modern language, which breathes more of a solid, scriptural, rational Piety, than the Common Prayer of the Church of England. And though the main of it was compiled considerably more than two hundred years ago, yet is the language of it, not only pure, but strong and elegant in the highest degree.*
>
> —*John Wesley, Preface to The Sunday Service of the Methodists in North America, September 9, 1784*

When John Wesley developed a ritual for Methodists in America to use on Sunday mornings as a weekly anchor to the more "expressive" worship forms they practiced in their society meetings on Sunday evenings, he gave them a version of the 1662 Book of Common Prayer with, as he put it, "little alteration." The alterations were relatively few, indeed. He deleted the lengthy "Commination" that was to be read by the priest prior to celebrating Holy Communion. He modified the burial ritual, eliminating reference to "a sure and certain hope." He replaced the Nicene Creed with the Apostles' Creed. He changed the rubric at the collection of alms to indicate the "basons" would be "placed upon the Table" rather than "humbly presented and placed upon the holy Table." He did not provide for a rite of Confirmation as such. He adapted the Psalter, editing or deleting those psalms deemed "highly improper for the mouths of a Christian congregation." And he eliminated many of the "holy days" listed, while generally retaining the readings from the BCP lectionary, as "at present answering no valuable end." The ritual he provided for American Methodists was otherwise nearly identical to what he himself would have used in the usual rounds of worship in the Church of England.

Indeed, if he or another Anglican priest were leading this ritual, one might not have been able to distinguish its flavor from the typical worship of an Anglican parish. As a ritual text, and presumably, Wesley intended, as a liturgical text *performed* by a worshiping assembly with its ordained presider, nothing in its essential character was altered. It was still, as Wesley put it, "pure. . . strong and elegant in the highest degree."

For Wesley, Anglican priest as well as Methodist, "strong" and "elegant" were important descriptors of what Anglican ritual was. I think he would say the same of the 1979 Book of Common Prayer for Episcopalians today.

Why "strong and elegant?" And why did Mr. Wesley especially commend the Anglican rite for Sunday morning use by Methodists in North America?

Though he is not here to answer these questions, I believe it is possible to guess responsibly. An important function of Anglican worship was to "impress," that is to form Christian character and basic Christian theology in the bodies and minds of its participants. Its mode was not generally that of convincing or exhorting, or even of moving the heart through emotional appeal. Rather, Anglican worship was designed to make an indelible imprint of Christian virtue and belief upon its participants by modeling and bodily rehearsing them in ritual community through repeated actions, common prayers printed in a prayer book for all to read or see, impressive pageantry and music, all offered in fairly dramatic worship space. Through the sheer beauty of its ritual actions and texts, holiness was impressed.

And, in my observation, this remains the case among Episcopalians today. What I offer in support of this claim is, in good Methodist fashion, testimonial.

I have been on a sojourn alongside the Episcopal Church for more than thirty years. I was raised as a Southern Baptist, but there were no Southern Baptist congregations at Kenyon College, the Episcopal-related liberal arts college in central Ohio where I was a student. At the invitation of friends, I began attending Harcourt Parish as a freshman and, strange and awkward as it was at first, grew to love the liturgy. While completing the MDiv at Southern Baptist Theological Seminary in Louisville, I led a small group praying for the mission of the church in Morning Prayer every weekday from the Book of Common Prayer for three years. During that time I was a member of a Southern Baptist congregation while also attending a Saturday evening Eucharist and healing service at a nearby Episcopal congregation. Today I am a United Methodist bureaucrat and liturgical scholar married to an Episcopal priest.

I have continued to find in my experiences of Episcopal worship a deep attentiveness to elegance and graciousness of both speech and movement. Processions are stately, not slow, but with a measured pace and dignity. Scriptures are read with attentiveness to the weight of their phrasing and how each word and phrase may be heard. Prayers are offered, whether by clergy or by laity, with a gravitas at once solemn and joyous. Preaching is often offered, in Wesley's terms for the liturgy itself, in what one might call a "solid. . . rational Piety," drawing more from the sensibility and energy of the liturgy overall than seeking to "drive" or persuade the congregation to do or believe anything the liturgy does not already "impress" in its prayers, hymns, and ritual actions.

The Eucharist marks the place where the elegant, impressive nature of Episcopal ritual is particularly noticeable to this "outsider." All that has been described about the rest of the liturgy remains in play. The words of the Eucharistic Prayer are offered with a kind of stable gravitas infused by solemn joy. The movements of the presider are at once measured and simple, each action (movement to *orans*, blessing the bread and cup, fraction, etc.) being given its time with no sense of haste or rush.

But perhaps most noticeable of all to me has been the bowing. Bowing happens at other points in the liturgy, whether as a processional cross passes by, or at certain words in the Nicene Creed or during the *Sanctus*, or, for some, at the name of Jesus. But at the Eucharist proper, the frequency of bowing seems to increase dramatically. Servers and assistants bow to the presider. The presider bows to the servers in return. This action of simple deference is repeated in what appears to be a matter of course, unpretentiously, at several points along the way, from the preparation of the table, to the washing of the hands of the presider, to the resetting of the table after all are served and the time for the prayer after the Eucharist has come. Perhaps the increase in the frequency of the bowing in these moments correlates with the holiness the Eucharist itself is understood both to require and to convey. Whatever the reasons, the increase in bowing at the Eucharist is one more means by which Episcopal liturgy impresses or imprints the minds and bodies of its participants with an ethos of elegance and an aesthetic of the holiness of beauty.

Strong, bold words, elegant actions, and a greater emphasis on impression than expression form the distinctive, delicious flavor of Episcopal worship and of an unmistakably Episcopal way of Christian life. In all things, many of the Episcopalians and nearly all of the Episcopal clergy I have known have been marked by a manner that is eloquent, measured, and gracious, both in their words and in the movement of their bodies. When their worship embodies these values, this ethos and this aesthetic of elegance, to Episcopalians it is holy because that is what beauty feels like.

Imagining United Methodist and Episcopal Holiness in the Beauty of Full Communion

Early American Methodist Episcopalians and Protestant Episcopalians, as each was known in the late eighteenth century, may have had little use for each other. The Methodists here, by and large, were "patriots" by US standards, while many, if not most, of the Episcopalians were at least suspected to be Tories. In 1784, John Wesley permitted the American Methodists to separate from the Church of England and become an independent church. The Methodist Episcopal Church, formed in December of that year, thus became the master of its own forms of organization and worship, no longer requiring its members to attend the Sunday morning services of Anglican parishes. By the time the Protestant Episcopal Church became autocephalous in 1789, it already had at least five years of living and worshiping without the "expressive" demands of the Methodists on its parishes, people, and priests. Within eight years, in 1792, the Methodist Episcopalians would, in effect, delete much of the liturgy Mr. Wesley had bequeathed, except for the rites at which only elders or bishops were expected to preside (Holy Communion proper, Baptism, Marriage, Burial, and Ordination). This action enabled Methodist Episcopal congregations, who at that time may have had an ordained elder available to them once per quarter, to offer a simpler form of Sunday morning worship led by laity, a form more in keeping with the expressive, ex tempore patterns they had known in their society meetings.

In the increasingly competitive church "market" that was early America, the distinctions between impressive Anglican worship and expressive Methodist worship became a basis for further division and distinction between our two churches. Methodists who seemed "too Episcopalian" were frowned on by their fellow Methodists, just as Episcopalians whose inclinations may have seemed more expressive may have been looked upon with some suspicion by their fellow Episcopalians.

Thus, what may have been experienced by the Wesleys and the Anglicans who comprised the bulk of early Methodism as a truly delicious opportunity to experience the fullness of the flavors of both through separate venues of worship (Methodist society meeting and Anglican congregation), has become for many of their Anglican and Methodist spiritual descendents a practice of commending our own flavors as "the one right recipe" while dismissing (or sometimes dissing!) the other as not quite fitting for our palates, or, in the worst cases, of the palates of any "true" or "civilized" Christian.

For both of our churches, always, Christian worship and life have been about beauty and holiness, whether the beauty of holiness worship expressively strives to exhort, or the holiness of the "beauty of the Lord" worship elegantly impresses.

What might be more beautiful or more holy than a relationship of full communion between United Methodists and Episcopalians in which both of our churches, each enacting its own ways of worship and Christian life in full integrity, actively encourage our own members to taste at its full strength, and learn also to cherish, the delicious flavor of the other?

Let me suggest what this does not mean. It does not mean any attempt to blend the worship of the two nor to act as if the differences in our approach to and embodiment of worship—our unique flavors—either did not exist or were insubstantial. Neither mélange nor mere toleration is a good way to bring us to the fuller beauty, the richer holiness, our full communion could offer our two churches. Expressive *and* impressive, driven *and* measured, exhortatory *and* elegant do not live together easily, or maybe even well, in the same ritual space, much less in the same ritual. The two flavors we bring may not be complementary if eaten together. Blending the two is likely to generate more incoherence and dissonance than beauty or joy. Ignoring these differences means ignoring what counts for beauty and holiness for each of us, and thus eviscerates rather than enlivens the worship either of us could offer whether separately or together.

But we all know from our own culinary experiences that flavors at very different ends of the spectra can, when eaten separately, each bring great enjoyment and an overall enrichment to our lives. We might not normally (or ever) eat Thai and Mexican food at one sitting. To me, at least, this would not seem a very promising "fusion" experience. In attempting such a combination, I imagine I may find one or the other distracting, annoying, or cloying, or the two together less than appetizing overall.

Yet I regularly find great value in each when I enjoy them in different times and places. And in enjoying each, separately, I find my appreciation for each on its own terms, as well as my range of appreciation for other cuisines, deepened and widened at once. I have come to find both delicious, and appreciate the flavor of each, and others, even more.

Perhaps this is the opportunity our full communion offers our two churches. What if we were to develop intentional processes of invitation to participate, at different times, in the worship and life of the other? What if, for example, a cadre of United Methodists, such as a Sunday School class, may be invited by both congregations to worship for the season of Advent with a local Episcopal congregation? What if a formation group from an Episcopal congregation were invited by both churches to spend a month with a United Methodist congregation for a particular sermon series or other special emphasis? And then, what if this process were intentionally repeated over time, so each congregation was sending and receiving persons from the other for a month, season, or series at a time, with the goal that as many in each congregation who wished would be able to have one or two "extended stays" with the other in worship and community life each year?

Some may decide from such an experience not to make such a sojourn again. That is fine. Not everyone may appreciate the emotional rigor of Methodist expressiveness or the measured elegance (or physical workout!) of Episcopal worship, any more than everyone may appreciate the escalating heat of Thai or the savory chilies of Mexican cuisine. Not everything is delicious to everyone. The beauty of one's own way of Christian worship and life abides.

But for those that do find such an exchange, an extended immersion in the flavors of the holiness of beauty, or the beauty of holiness, to be pleasing in itself, imagine what may be opened up. The expressive may find also the value of measured solemnity. The elegant may discover the joy of being driven to action, or tears. Holiness may be found in beautiful worship, and beauty in holy living. Measured elegance may find the value of striving, and those striving, the value of directing their efforts toward beauty as much as truth.

I do not know if I will have occasion to return to the Chinese buffet in Kinshasa. But I do know I love Congolese food, as well as the Chinese food I have eaten in San Francisco, New York, Philadelphia, and in the Midwest, each with its own unique twists brought from local or traditional sources. I would testify it is all delicious.

May our two churches, as we move toward and into full communion, find ways to express and impress upon our own lives, and with each other, the unmistakable, delicious, and distinctive flavors of holiness as we have come to find it, beautifully.

The Reverend Dr. Taylor W. Burton-Edwards is
Director of Worship Resources for the General Board
of Discipleship of the United Methodist Church.

CHAPTER 5

Theology and Practice

Commentary on Sections 3.5, 3.6, and 3.7 of "A Theological Foundation for Full Communion between The Episcopal Church and The United Methodist Church"

William O. Gregg

Introduction

The task of this chapter is to look *theologically* at issues and questions raised explicitly or implicitly in Sections 3.5–3.7, and to identify and to make suggestions for further attention and work. The commentary offered here is that of an Episcopal Church bishop and theologian, and it seems fair and appropriate to acknowledge this up front. In general, the document is offered as a *theological* document. In these sections, however, the focus is largely on practices. Practices are either the result of theological understandings and insights, or they are the objects of theological reflection. Either pole is a legitimate starting point. Methodologically, these sections begin with practices. Yet, the next step, developing adequately the inherent theology is missing.

While these sections fairly clearly lay out the United Methodist practices, from the Episcopal side, there needs to be a fuller identification of practices and how these lead to theological understandings. At present, the section lacks an appropriate balance of presentation that gives a fulsome picture of the starting point for theological work. Both the Episcopal Church (TEC) and the United Methodist Church (UMC) need to do further work in breadth and depth on the theology of these practices, for the sake of both our churches in order for the dialogue to progress and to provide the appropriate, adequate theological bases that this document sets out to provide for the discernment and decisions that will need to be made.

3.5 Understandings of the Historic Episcopate

Section 3.5 identifies understandings of both churches, names issues, and suggests ways forward in the process of coming to full communion (definition, Introduction, p. 1) with each other. This section devotes a paragraph to the development and tradition of the historic episcopate, a paragraph on the understanding of the Episcopal Church, and then two-plus pages of the understanding and practice of the United Methodist Church. There is a serious lack of balance of presentation at a level of appropriate depth and thoroughness to address an essential and complex issue, the historic episcopate, from the perspectives of both churches. Theological references are largely absent, and what literature is cited is largely United Methodist. Both the Episcopal Church and the United Methodist Church need to do much more work in breadth of research, depth of thinking, and balance of presentation (dialogical structure) with regard to the office and ministry of bishop.

It is unclear what we are to take away from the opening part of this section. The language names the historic episcopate as merely a "precedent." Both partners of the dialogue need to present a more fully developed theological understanding of the term "precedent," why that word was chosen, and on what theological basis the word is appropriate in this instance. There needs to be further discussion on the tradition of the episcopal order in the history of the church. A well thought-out, developed theology of ordination and orders, especially episcopacy, accompanied by an equally well thought-out theology of priesthood (TEC) and Elder (UMC), and the Order of deacon is also needed. All three orders are inextricably a part of a fulsome and adequate theological understanding and *praxis* of the historic episcopate and apostolic succession.

The ordering of the life and work of the church in its ordained leadership and sacramental life according to what we may call "catholic polity," *viz.*, the historic episcopate, priests, and deacons, was, from very early in the church until the sixteenth century, the way the church ordered itself. It was not merely "precedent," which I understand at least to imply one option among others. There can be many precedents for many things. Many questions are thus raised that deserve extended consideration within this TEC/UMC dialogue. Is this section implicitly giving priority of place to post-Reformation polity and the ordering of ordained ministry? Or, is the point that, post-Reformation, catholic polity is one option among several, all of which are of equal value and legitimacy? Or is this the set-up for the lengthy discussion of United Methodist polity and practices with regard to orders? What are the theologies reflected in the understanding of episcopacy presented here? What are the impacts of these theologies for each church in the context of a potential relationship of full communion? The discussion here is of *polity* and ways in which polity has changed in both TEC and the UMC. But, again, there is unfortunately no theology here, and that has rendered the consideration of ways forward to be mechanical or technical adjustments to the structure(s) (polity). Using the current actual praxis as a starting point for discussion is a good place to start. However, in a document purporting to be a *theological* foundation for a major decision in both our churches, the praxis of each church must be accompanied by a thorough theological examination.

The paragraph addressing episcopacy in the Episcopal Church is superficial, and does not grasp the depth and importance of the episcopal tradition in the history of the church or the Anglican tradition. The arguments would be greatly strengthened if they were fully annotated. Lacking annotation, the paragraph on the Episcopal Church lacks credibility, reading like assertions without foundation. Those who now go forward to consider full communion need to spend a great deal of time carefully studying and thinking about the role and function of the historic episcopate in the Anglican tradition and why it is identified as an essential of the church for Episcopalians.[1] Again, utilizing a dialogical structure of presentation, it would be helpful for the UMC to offer a more extensive account of the historical and current practices with their theological underpinnings.

It is interesting that there are no references to the Ordinals of either denomination. Certainly, for Episcopalians, the ordination prayers are key primary texts for our theology and understanding, as well as practice, of Holy Orders. Under the ancient rubric, *lex orandi, lex cedendi*, it seems essential that careful study of and reflection on the Ordinals, particularly the prayers of ordination (and consecration) and attendant rubrics, are need to establish clearly what the operative theologies of ordination in general and of the specific orders are.[2] This is necessary

---

1 See, *Chicago-Lambeth Quadrilateral* 1886/88; Book of Common Prayer, 876–77.
2 I would add, especially from the TEC perspective, that it would also be necessary to look at the Baptismal Covenants, given the baptismal ecclesiology of TEC. Baptism forms the larger ecclesiological and sacramental context for the theology and practice of ordained ministries in general, and here, of the episcopate in particular.

for an appropriate, rich discussion in the churches about whether and how the mutual, full recognition of our orders can occur and what our orders would/might look like going forward.

On the Methodist side, in the two pages addressing the UMC history and practices, much more wrestling with the theology and ethics of Wesley's actions and rationalizations for his theology and practices of ordination could provide theological understandings and critical perspectives. Episcopalians and Methodists need to address substantively the marked differences of theology and practice articulated and enacted by Wesley and his followers; how that continues to play out in the UMC today; and, what these differences mean in relation to the history, theology, and practices of TEC. Are these practices and theologies compatible to a degree that allows for mutual recognition? Here TEC experiences with both the Evangelical Lutheran Church in America (ELCA) and the Moravians may provide some framework for the questions and conversations. There is, from an Episcopalian perspective, a curious thread that runs through this section on the Methodist side that, in their language, revolves around an understanding of "emergency" and a consequent practice of exceptionalist thinking or determination of when there was an "emergency." (p. 28, 29) One also has to wonder at the facile acceptance of Wesley's notion of a "right" to ordain. (p. 28) Further explication of and thinking about the notion of "presbyterial succession" (n. 49, p. 29) in the understanding of apostolic succession, historic episcopate, and the role and function of bishops is necessary.

Going forward, further discussion of this section would benefit, I think, from engaging the ELCA/TEC document "Called to Common Mission" (CCM), for deepening the understanding and theological underpinning of the historic episcopate in a situation where one of the dialogue partners is not in the historic succession. CCM also provides specific insights and ways forward in mutually recognizing the orders of each church where there are and continue to be different theologies and practices. There seems to be an assumption that being ordained "superintendent" was and is equivalent to being ordained and consecrated a bishop; however, it is not clear that this is the case theologically, nor is it clear in what ways it may be the case.

Given the historical language in Methodism, an examination of the position of "district superintendent" would also be relevant, both in terms of the ordering/structuring of the church and ministry in relation to the conference bishop. Are there, in the Methodist mind, episcopal dimensions, authority, or other relationship to episcopal office, roles, and functions? From the perspective of the Episcopal Church, the district superintendent's ministry shares characteristics administratively and pastorally with a bishop suffragan. Would full communion bring with it a new understanding and practice for the UMC that builds on their current practices, for example, to make district superintendents bishops suffragan? Might this not also be an opportunity for TEC to come to new forms and practices of episcopacy? For both churches, the issues of jurisdiction, authority, and function of the diocesan/conference bishop, and in TEC, bishops coadjutor, suffragan, and assistant may provide some creative new insights and practices for both churches as the roles, functions, and authority (jurisdiction) of district superintendents and bishops is examined.

A major opportunity for further work comes from the Methodist implication that (legitimate) episcopacy is (can be) *sui generis* (an "emergency"?) within a denomination as long as it is rationalized into being in continuity with the idea of "apostolic succession." It seems to me that it needs to be far more clear and explicit what the theological relationship is between the "historic episcopate" and "apostolic succession" on the one hand, and the theological reasons for how and why the episcopacy in catholic polity is the primary historic bearer and symbol of the content and meaning of apostolic succession. There needs to be clarity around the focused nature of the *office* of bishop as bearer of apostolic tradition, even if in the exercise of the office by particular people throughout history, this function of episcopacy has been (mightily) obscured. The reliance on "Baptism, Eucharist, and Ministry" is not particularly helpful and gives only one, very Protestant read of episcopacy. I think the primary texts that need serious examination, especially the Ordinals, would provide a stronger and more helpful foundation for theological understanding of our practices as we go forward.

Recent determinations notwithstanding, including CCM, the office or order of bishop has, historically, been a kind of guarantor of "apostolic succession." Recent practice and theology has tended to reduce the bishop to a convenient "sign" ("a precedent") but not real symbol, "guarantor," or guardian of apostolicity in any material sense. These terms are somewhat murky and offer to enhance our understanding and the clarity of our theology through further conversation about their theological meaning. Moreover, such a rendering of "apostolic succession" and the episcopate, both from the perspective of catholic tradition and Anglican tradition bears some real theological examination in light of the description of the bishop's ministry as "one called to be one with the apostles" and "to guard the faith, unity, and discipline of the church." (BCP, 517) What is at stake theologically and practically is more than what "Baptism, Eucharist, and Ministry" offers in its consideration of the episcopacy. What is reflected in this document is the same confusion (found in "Baptism, Eucharist, and Ministry") of *office* with *particular holders* of the office as ground for a theological conclusion or interpretation of episcopacy. What, theologically, is the difference between being the "guarantor" and/or "guardian of the faith, unity, and discipline of the church" and "sign"? Are these questions of the office of bishop or simply questions of the person who holds that office? What is the relationship of person (and his/her character) to the office and its character?

Simply to make a distinction between "historic episcopacy" and "apostolic succession" is inadequate. In the particular instance of the Episcopal Church and the United Methodist Church, what does this mean theologically, and what are the implications for both polity and *praxis*? It is noteworthy, and of concern, that this document does not address the *praxis* of episcopacy in either church. They are, in fact, quite different, and bear our careful, thoughtful examination. For example, UMC bishops have only a role that could be described as "observer" in General Conference, whereas, in TEC, the House of Bishops is an equal partner with the House of Deputies in the legislative process of decision-making at General Convention. Additionally, some attention needs to be given to the role of bishop as "chief pastor." Again, Methodist and Episcopal bishops function very differently. This difference of function reflects different understandings of the roles and meaning of bishop, as office and as person, and of the church.

More careful study needs to be given to the development of the episcopacy in the Episcopal Church and in the UMC. The paragraph devoted to this topic (p. 29f.) oversimplifies in its effort to establish commonalities in the history of our two churches. It again seems to be an unbalanced statement listing considerably to the Methodist experience and understanding. The opportunity for the dialogue and our churches is that the "dots" identified here need to be properly connected with deep explication, thoughtful analysis by each church and in the dialogue committee in order to produce clearer and more accurate understandings theologically and historically.

In the second section, "The Issues: Distinctions between 'Historic Succession' and 'Apostolic Succession,'" the opening paragraph is confusing and confused. While it is certainly a legitimate point to make, *viz.*, that no ecclesial body can or ought rightly to make judgments of the validity of another ecclesial body's orders (or anything else), this is not the question at hand. This paragraph simply goes nowhere. The paragraph becomes less clear as it moves from the matter of validity to the notions of "reconciliation" and "recognition." How are these three concepts connected? The issue of validity, which needs to be named and explicitly explicated, is one of jurisdiction. No church has jurisdiction over another (*Apostolicæ curæ* notwithstanding). The question that needs asking is something like this: "Do we see in the orders of each other's church what is necessary to recognize those orders as fulfilling the meaning and purpose of each order?" Again, as this was an important question in the ELCA/TEC dialogues leading to CCM, it would be useful to ask the question, "How might what we learned and concluded there, be helpful in this dialogue?" This was also an important question in the TEC/Moravian dialogue, both around episcopacy and the diaconate.

Passing comment is made noting the Chicago-Lambeth Quadrilateral, but the meaning and importance of item four of the Quadrilateral is simply left lying there without substantive comment or engagement. The fourth point on the historic episcopate in the Quadrilateral is a very dense one that needs to be teased out and thought about deeply and carefully by both TEC and the UMC. It is not simply the name of a functional office or a structure of polity. It is a theological conclusion, and, as with all such conclusions, needs to be unpacked carefully.

The ministries of "commissioned ministers" or variations thereof in the UMC and the celebration of the sacraments offers an interesting opportunity for serious thinking and discussion between and within our churches.[3] Bracketing Baptism, for which there is an historical and time-honored tradition in the church of provision for emergency Baptism by anyone, Christian or not, who baptizes with water in the name of the Trinity intending to do what the church intends, the matter of orders and so-called lay-presidency needs much more careful and detailed work. I mention this here as it is related to the ministry of the bishop as ordinary, but will write more fully on this in the next section.

"Ways Forward" relies essentially on a paragraph from "Baptism, Eucharist, and Ministry" (1982). One may argue whether this paragraph is correct in claiming that the episcopate and "the transmission of the Gospel" are two separate ways of sustaining apostolic succession. It

---

3 These comments here and later are made in the context of this document. Legislation was brought to the 2012 General Conference to change this practice by ordaining those designated as "commissioned ministers" as elders. This would effectively eliminate this particular issue and clearly establish the norm of ordained persons presiding at the Eucharist. The status of that legislation, as well as the text and the consideration at General Conference will need the attention of both denominations going forward. However, that legislation was not adopted. Therefore, the issue remains a serious one going forward.

would be helpful going forward for the dialogue teams and our churches
to revisit *BEM*, particularly the section on episcopacy and succession
(historic and apostolic), to make a full, critical examination of the theology, ecclesiology, and practice argued in *BEM*. There are those of
the Patristic Period, such as Ignatius of Antioch, who did not see apostolic succession and historic succession as two separate tracks. Rather,
he understood a unified, singular apostolic succession for which the historic succession in the office of bishop was the instrument of the apostolicity of the church. Arguing as he did that the bishop is essential to the
church ("where the Bishop is, the Church is"), it would follow that the
transmission of the Gospel was at least principally transmitted through
the office of bishop as embodied in a particular place at a particular
time in a particular person. Historically, the teaching office, as well as
preaching, has been a fundamental ministry of the bishop.

The bullet-point statements at the end of the section (pp. 31f.) invite
further careful theological work and development. The first item is
both vague and defensive. The language of the necessity to develop
"ways to recognize and reconcile the two episcopacies . . . not to call
into question the authenticity of each other's ordinations" (p. 31) really
needs a fulsome theological explication within the dialogue and for the
church-wide discussions in each denomination. Some thought might
also be given to what difference it might make if the two episcopacies cannot be found, at this time, to be recognized or reconcilable.
The question, in any case, is not of "authenticity" of ordinations. It is
a question of whether the theological understanding of each church is
such that each can recognize in the other's orders the fullness of each
order. This does require both clarity of theological understanding and
articulation as well as practice, and ultimately a judgment by Methodists
and Episcopalians about what they see and hear. Are we doing the same
thing to a degree that supports mutual recognition? Or, are we using
the same terminology, but intending and meaning things quite different
(or insufficiently substantively the same) so that, from the perspective of
each church, we cannot affirm that the other does and means what we
do and mean through Holy Orders, and episcopacy in particular?

Point 3, on the ongoing reforming dynamic of the episcopate, may
be true, as far as it goes, but needs careful theological examination and
explication to be most useful to both churches in their discernment
and decision-making processes. What does it mean that the historic
episcopate "is always in a process of reform"? How? By what process,
criteria, and authority? What are the possibilities and limits of this
ongoing reforming and development? How does this dynamic embody

the Anglican concept of "locally adapted"?[4] Throughout consideration of this dimension of the espiscopate, Episcopalians and Methodist will benefit from the wisdom of Richard Hooker and his caution to his own day in *Lawes of Ecclesiastical Politie*. Recognizing this inherent dynamic of change and development (ongoing reform), he reminds us that such change is properly thoughtful, prayerful, and cautious. The reality of change is inevitable; however, it is never to be change merely for the sake of change or for what is merely new and different. It must honor the tradition, even in radical discontinuity with it, and it must be argued and articulated that it is better for the good of God's people.

Point 4, on the colonial adaptation of the episcopate by both churches, is arguably inaccurate, and too broadly stated. Certainly from the Episcopal side, the matter would not, historically, be framed in terms of simply adapting a structure "for the sake of mission." The fact that it took several years to work things out in the Episcopal Church suggests that the matter is far more complicated and subtle, as a matter of polity and theological understanding of church, God's mission, and ministries (lay and ordained).

This document, as a whole, seeks to articulate a theological foundation for full communion between our two churches. However, at the end of this section, as it now stands, there is not a theological foundation for the episcopate that will support either church making such a profound and important decision either about the orders in each church or about full communion.

3.6 Practices Related to Presidency at the Eucharist

Section 3.6 focuses on practices, devotes most of its attention to UMC practices, gives little attention to the nearly universal norm that presiding at sacraments is a ministry of bishops and priests, and provides no substantial exploration of sacramental theology. There is a clear confusion between "practice" and "theology" as such.

A principal theological matter not addressed is, to use the language of the Roman Church, a theology of "faculties" that could provide a theological framework for both TEC and the UMC. This is not to say that such a theology is appropriate, but if one is going to talk about "authorizing" persons to do specific priestly ministries restricted to specific communities, something like a theology of faculties, serious difficulties

---

4 Chicago-Lambeth Quadrilateral; Book of Common Prayer, 876–77.

notwithstanding, it is necessary to thinking this practice through theologically. Otherwise, you end up with something like what seems to me to be the Methodist position of quasi-clerical/lay persons ("commissioned ministers") who act, essentially, as "mass priests" in their congregation. I would observe that the medieval church tried this and it failed miserably, leaving both a corrupted and diminished sacramental life and priesthood, from which it took much time to recover.

Is it reasonable to extend roles and functions piecemeal, under any circumstances? What are the theological and practical consequences of such a fragmentation for deacon, priest/elder, and bishop and the sacramental life of the church? What does such fragmentation mean for the relationship of each order to the other and to orders as a whole? Who has the authority to authorize or license the functions (faculties) and on what theological basis? What are the faculties (fragments) and who decides what these faculties are and on what basis? In this context, the matter of who properly presides at the Eucharist can be addressed and invites a robust conversation.

The Methodist position seems to want to straddle both sides of the fence simultaneously without a compelling theological and liturgical grounding. The chief rubric for their ambivalence and ambiguity seems to be exceptions to the norm for eucharistic presidency and a form of the notion of "emergency" and Wesley's own sense of the "right" to ordain. (Sec. 3.5, p. 28) It seems to be a "We need/want to do this, therefore, we have a 'right' to do so." stance. And, indeed, they may be right, within the UMC. However, in the context of this dialogue, much more theological thinking and explication by both UMC and TEC members needs to be done. As it is, I think it is very difficult for an Episcopalian to embrace the Methodist position. Their reluctance to state clearly and with commitment the normative Christian practice since very early in the tradition only further makes their position more untenable on the roles and meaning of "commissioned ministers" and sacramental ministry within the church.

What does it mean to claim that the UMC "commissioned ministers" (and "local pastors"?) receive "Episcopal appointment, licensing, and conference authorization" to preside at the sacraments and that this "functions as *a kind of ordination*" (italics mine). (See p. 33) There is only a weak expression of the norm for presiding at Eucharist, and then, it seems, as with episcopacy, to be merely a "precedent"—one option among others, depending on what its deemed necessary or urgent or an emergency in a given situation to do what they want to do in that place, among these people, at this time. (p. 32) We see the same problem in Sec.

3.4, entitled, "The Relationship Between Baptism and the Reception of Holy Communion." (p. 25f.) The absence here of a Methodist articulation of a clear and coherent theology of ordination and of normative standards, definitions, roles, and meanings of the orders is exacerbated by the confusion between the roles of those in orders and laity, specifically that of the laity and the diaconate with relation to the sacramental life of the church.

A clear theology of sacraments and ordination, with a clear differentiation among the Orders, as well as a theology of the relationship among the ministries of all the baptized, is needed here from both churches. As with episcopacy, it is impossible for either church to make a decision together or separately on the basis of this document as it stands now. The appeal to the ELCA needs both to be documented and explicated. Here it simply reads as a form of "They authorize lay presidency, so we can." Such a stance completely begs the question theologically, sacramentally, and ecclesiologically, not to mention its implications for full communion. And yet, there is actually a wonderful opportunity here for conversation, formation, and teaching in the dialogue committee and in our two churches. It would be my hope that we take full advantage of it.

In "The Issues" section (p. 33) it is noted that in TEC presiding at the Eucharist has "always been restricted to bishops and priests." It is further noted that attempts to authorize "lay presidency" has consistently met with nearly universal and strong counsel within the Anglican Communion not to do so.[5] Two sentences, and we move on to the UMC paragraph which focuses only on the pragmatic by framing the question in terms of making "sacraments available to congregations served by local pastors." That matter is a pastoral and practical issue, and one properly grounded in a well-developed theology of sacrament and orders. The appeal to TEC's experiment with "Canon 9 priests," is, apparently, (another) precedent for the UMC practice. The parallel might work if the UMC General Conference makes all lay pastors and "commissioned ministers" elders.[6] And, as TEC discovered, the issues of formation, education, and training are serious matters with profound

---

5 One of the things that needs to be said from the TEC side is that by and large, if not entirely, the efforts to institute "lay presidency" has originated in very evangelical, protestant areas of the Anglican Communion. As especially the case with the leading proponent, the Australian Diocese of Sydney, it has been tainted with regional politics and a summary rejection of the catholic principles of Anglicanism built upon a somewhat militant, evangelical Protestantism seasoned with a high level of individualism and presumed sense of absolute autonomy.
6 There was a proposal brought to the 2012 General Conference to make all "commissioned ministers" (lay pastors) elders. Unfortunately the proposal was not adopted.

consequences, which must also be examined and dealt with both theologically and practically.

While making an implicit argument that "commissioned ministers" are at least something like the former Canon III.9 ("locally ordained priest") provisions of TEC, it would be helpful to the dialogue for TEC to explain why we ultimately concluded that both as a matter of theology and of practice, the "Canon 9 priest" was not sustainable, and has been removed. A two-tiered priesthood presented pastoral and professional issues, and undermined the theology of priesthood in numerous ways, especially the Anglican and Methodist understanding that one is ordained priest/elder for the church, not a specific community within which priesthood is restricted. Additionally, TEC does not have a sacramental theology that supports this restricted ministry. The issue of presidency is *theological* first, and then only is it practical and pastoral. Practice without the appropriate theological underpinning nearly always does damage to the integrity of the church, and to the ministries of lay and ordained alike, and in this case to the sacramental life and spiritual welfare of God's people.

I think that it would be helpful for TEC and the UMC to situate this question of lay presidency, which is more academic that practical, within the context of a larger theological conversation about Baptism, the People of God, and how, theologically and practically, the Body of Christ functions in its love and service of the Lord (ministries). The question moves in two directions: (1) the internal ordering of the body for its life and work, and (2) the outward movement of God's people in love and service (ministries) in the Name of Jesus. Both of these matters fall within the context of the larger understanding of the church and the Mission of God, which each of us and our ministries serve. Hence, Section 3.6 is directly related both to the previous section on episcopacy and the following section on lay ministries.

After the work of several decades to articulate an understanding of church, the People of God, and ministries (ordained and non-ordained) grounded in Baptism, the TEC position is clear: all ministry is grounded in and derivative of Baptism. Relative to this understanding as a fundamental biblical image of the church is found in St. Paul's metaphor of the church as the Body of Christ (1 Corinthians 12, Romans 12), into which we are initiated through Baptism. Within this context, we quickly see that St. Paul was clear that the Body of Christ is differentiated within itself, according to the gifts of the Spirit. (See Ephesians 4 and 1 Corinthians 12–13.) One of the ways the Body is internally differentiated is in its ordering of ministries. I think it is essential to understand from the beginning that there is a sense in which we are all lay persons, that is, *ho laós Theou* (*laós à laity*), the People of God, and through Baptism, we remain so. It is within the People of God that some are called to more specific ministries, *e.g.*, as ordained persons—bishop, priest, deacon. From the Pauline understanding, *all* of these "orders" are necessary and presuppose each other by definition. (cf. BCP [79], Catechism, "The Ministry," Q/A 1, p. 855) One is not "better" than another; each is different in the focus of its particular contribution to the life and work of the whole Body of Christ. I believe that to this point, there is substantial, if not complete, agreement between our churches.

The challenge comes in how we think about and practice being the Body of Christ. In this document, the theological questions and embodiments tend to focus more on the internal ordering of the church. It seems to me that there is essential agreement on ministries in the world that proclaim the Gospel and invite people to participate in the life and work of Christ through the church, Christ's Body. What is needed now is for both the UMC and TEC to articulate a clear and comprehensive theology of sacraments, orders, and laity, and how they and their ministries relate to one another. Is authorization to preside at Eucharist merely the delegation of authority to perform a task, or is it something more? Is presidency a matter of function only, or does it express an understanding of the church and the way the church orders itself to participate in God's Mission? Does the existence of a real or perceived "need" ("emergency"?) constitute necessary and sufficient grounds, theologically, to allow for lay presidency at the Eucharist? Even situating all ministry in the context of Baptism, does not such a stance blur the boundaries and definitions of the various orders within the church, and thereby reduce and confuse both sacraments and ministries as well as the good order of the church? I am put in mind here again of Paul's image of the Body of Christ. Each part is distinct and has its particular function and contribution to the life and working of the Body.

What do we say and mean if we simply regard presidency as a function which can be assigned (by the church) to anyone at any time on the basis of perceived or real need? It seems to me, particularly from the standpoint of norms, that such a position is non-defensible biblically, theologically, or liturgically.

If this understanding of presidency is to be the intended direction of this dialogue for our churches, that needs to be stated clearly and have a strong, clear theological foundation for consideration by the churches.

TEC needs to make a clear theological response from an Anglican perspective and be clear about whether or not TEC could endorse or live with such a direction. In this instance, it is also important that both denominations show a clear and greater understanding and appreciation of the norm of Christian tradition and the seriousness of this question and it implications.

3.7 Practices with Respect to the Laity

This section reduces a major, essential, and substantive topic to three very brief paragraphs. If there were ever a place where real and material commonalities were to be found between TEC and the UMC, and which unquestionably merit thoughtful and extended reflection, it is with regard to the ministries of the laity. As noted already, the Episcopal Church has come to ground the life and work of the church in Baptism. Hence, all ministries (lay and ordained) of all the People of God (*laós Theou*) are grounded in Baptism. An opportunity has been missed here to explore robustly the ecclesiology of St. Paul in Romans 12 and 1 Corinthians 12—the Body of Christ. Yet, it is not an opportunity gone. It will be very important to explore fully a Body of Christ ecclesiology in terms both of St. Paul's image (1 Corinthians 12 and Romans 12) and in terms of the baptismal liturgies of the Book of Common Prayer (1979) and the *United Methodist Hymnal* (1989).

The language here makes rather loose use of the technical term "office," and one is not certain exactly what constitutes an "office." Licensed ministry, for example, of lay reader or eucharistic visitor is not (ordinarily) termed an "office" in any of the liturgical churches. (See Canon III.4) Rather, the term ordinarily references Holy Orders (the office of bishop, priest, or deacon) or one of the liturgies of the hours (in TEC, the Daily Offices: Morning Prayer, Noonday Prayer, Evening Prayer, Compline). It would be helpful not to clericalize, even implicitly, the laity or their ministries, as "office" suggests. A review of TEC Canons III.1–9 and the parallel sections of the UMC *Book of Discipline* by the dialogue committee, with theological reflection, interpretations and conclusions, along with suggestions going forward, would be helpful for both denominations, especially in the larger church-wide discussions of full communion between us.

The document does note in the section, "Ways Forward" that licensed ministries are "ones which enrich our lives as churches, and [we] do not see them as problematic as we move towards full communion." (p. 34) Perhaps. Given the vagaries and ambiguities of the section "Lay

Presidency at the Eucharist" and the apparent willingness of the United Methodist Church to license on some form of "as needed" or "emergency" or "urgent" basis, it is difficult to tell, from an Episcopal perspective, whether or not the claim is supported by the facts. Certainly the attention to the polity of the Episcopal Church, even the reference to Canon III.1, is slight. The licensed ministries of Canon III.4 for lay persons neither includes nor suggests that these ministries include presiding at Eucharist, though, as throughout the Christian tradition, Baptism *in extremis* by a lay person is endorsed and recognized in TEC. (See BCP, p. 313) In the Episcopal Church, such Baptisms are recorded as soon as practicable in the appropriate parish register.

In a document entitled "A Theological Foundation. . . ", the absence of a well-developed, thoughtful theology of the laity and their ministries is surprising. Certainly "licensed ministries" is only a part, and a relatively small one at that, of lay ministries. "Commissioned ministers" and lay pastors in the UMC notwithstanding, ministries (lay and ordained), at least from both a TEC and the UMC perspectives, are about the life and work of the whole people of God as they fulfill their vows of the Baptismal Covenant in daily life. I think that with the further work needed in the previous two sections (Sec. 3.5 and 3.6), a more comprehensive theological analysis of lay ministries will enable a fuller and more robust theological analysis of the practices within both denominations. In considering the practices of our two denominations, it would be helpful to hold together the ministries of both lay and ordained persons. Ecclesially, they are equally necessary and important. Each presumes the other.

Being clear about what ministry is (=participation in the Mission of God) requires clarity about what the Mission of God is. Only then is it really possible for us to have the best, fullest, most robust, fruitful, constructive, and creative conversation about what it is we actually do organizationally to order our life and work (ministries) to and for God's Mission. Only then can we really tackle issues of how the ways each church orders itself aligns with God's Mission and then with each other. Then we can address, theologically and practically, the question of whether we see in each other what is necessary for full communion.

I have in this chapter sought to identify substantive matters, especially those that call for further and deeper consideration by TEC and the UMC. At times, the critique may have seemed sharp. That said, it seems to me that matters worth the kind of time, energy, and effort our two churches have and are giving to this dialogue and the pursuit of full communion deserve our fullest, most critical, and most faithful engagement and responses. The desire for full communion is a profound and extremely important matter, and much like marriage, ought not to be entered into "unadvisedly or lightly, but reverently, deliberately, and in accordance with the purposes for which it was instituted by God." (BCP, p. 423) The unity of the church is not without diversity of theologies and practices. Our unity is in the one Lord, one faith, one baptism, one God and Father of us all. Getting there is a matter of grace and the working of the Holy Spirit. This document of the TEC/UMC dialogue is a step along the way in a complex process of God's people seeking God's will and to be faithful in response to it. I do not think we are there yet. I do think that this is an important conversation for all of us and that this document marks an opportunity to continue in deeper theological conversations of our partnership under grace and empowered and enlightened by the Holy Spirit. Such mutual engagement and conversation can only accrue to the benefit of God's people as we discern, explore, and live into the grace and gifts of God to us.

Final Reflections

I am not certain that the unity of the church *qua* our oneness in Christ, must mean what the current definition of "full communion" means. Simply put, one way of interpreting the Pauline image of the Body of Christ would be to say that "full communion" or, in the older phrase, "organic communion" in the sense of all becoming one ecclesial body, means the recognition and reconciliation of all aspects of being church, even if we continue to call ourselves by different names. I think the COCU experiment demonstrates two things: (1) that "organic unity" is not viable, and (2) the concept misses the point of Paul's image and the theme of unity in the Fourth Gospel.

So, what if rather than trying to reconcile (whatever that may mean), for example, our theologies and practices of the episcopate, we agreed to say that we believe, acknowledge, affirm that each church is truly and fully a part of the Body of Christ, the Church, each being endowed by the Spirit with different experiences, gifts, and ways of living the Gospel and our baptismal vows. And yet, precisely because we are gifted differently by the Spirit, we believe that each church should continue, as a part of the Body of Christ, to function in its own particular ways. However, we fully recognize all persons who are baptized in the Name of the Trinity with water, and thereby sacramentally made a part of the Body of Christ and raised to the new life of grace, are unconditionally welcomed and received in each church at any celebration of the Eucharist and invited to participate fully, including receiving Holy Communion.

Moreover, as distinct parts of the one Body of Christ, we are committed to working collaboratively in various ministries of service in the world wherever and whenever possible.

Finally, we believe that what makes us one in Christ and therefore a distinct part of the one, whole, Body of Christ, the one, holy, catholic, and apostolic church is our Baptism and the continued working of the Spirit within and through us as individuals and as ecclesial bodies of which Christ is the head.

It seems to me that the idea that we all be one is an illusion to the extent that it does not honor the reality of differences and believes that unity and sameness are the same. Plato, bless his heart, got this wrong. Aristotle, and subsequently Paul, got it right. The more advanced and mature a body, the more internally differentiated it becomes precisely so that it can function in the maximally effective ways. I think, as a matter of faith and of theology, that we seriously err when we miss "denominationalism" as a gift of the Spirit and the task of the church. We equally seriously miss the mark when we fail to appreciate the differences and see, recognize, own, and participate in the work of the Spirit that binds us together as one body, with Christ as head.

In fact, I would argue that historically, the Anglican tradition is especially gifted to understand and support such an ecclesiology. We need look only at the BCP 1552 and the Words of Ministration for Communion (which has been retained since the sixteenth century)—it is clearly a case of simply joining the Conformist (Catholic) phrase to the presbyterian (Protestant) phrase, without explanation, but just letting it be. Biblically, this is not too dissimilar to the example of the two quite distinct Creation Narratives in Genesis 1–3. Or, in a culinary image, olive oil and balsamic vinegar do not mix because it is not of their nature, but when they are left alone together to be sopped up by a fine piece of bread, the differences are held together by the bread in a really tasty experience.

We agree, I think, on Who is our unity. The difficulty appears to be the *how* of realizing and maintaining that unity. Perhaps the question ultimately is a pneumatological one, and not an organizational or sacramental one.

The Right Reverend William O. Gregg, PhD, is VI
Bishop of Eastern Oregon (res.) and Assistant Bishop
in the Diocese of North Carolina.

CHAPTER 6

Response to "A Theological Foundation for Full Communion between The Episcopal Church and The United Methodist Church"

Ellen K. Wondra

I have been invited to reflect on the Righ Reverend William Gregg's discussion of "A Theological Foundation for Full Communion," in which he focuses on the sections on the historic episcopate, presidency at the Eucharist, and practices of lay ministry. I am most appreciative of Bishop Gregg's very close reading of "A Theological Foundation," and largely agree that there are matters touched on here that need much further theological and ecclesiological elaboration as part of the Episcopal Church's and Anglican Communion's response to Jesus's High Priestly Prayer "that they all may be one."

I also agree with Bishop Gregg in wanting more, and in wanting things put rather differently at many junctures in "A Theological Foundation." But I may not agree with Bishop Gregg about what is needed in order for the Episcopal Church and the United Methodist Church to move into a greater visible expression of the communion which we share in Christ.

The concerns that Bishop Gregg raises can, I think, be gathered into four general areas:

- The theological nature and ecclesiological importance of the historic episcopate, and the relation of theology, ecclesiology, and polity more broadly;

- The theology of the sacraments, especially the presence of Christ in the sacrament of Holy Communion;

75

- The theology of ministry including the interdependence of the baptized and the ordained, focused particularly by presidency at Holy Communion and the scope and significance of the ministry of the laity; and

- The grounds and evidence for making judgments about whether or not certain theological positions, ecclesiological orderings, and ecclesial practices are adequate to the Christian faith and appropriate bases for overcoming past divisions.

There is no question that each of these is a serious issue in ecumenical dialogue and agreement. Each one comes up over and over again in all of the Episcopal Church's and Anglican Communion's many bilateral, multilateral, and conciliar dialogues. Neither the Episcopal Church nor the Anglican Communion has claimed that it is so certain of its position on any of them as to exempt these topics from further conversation with other Christians.

In part this is because it appears to be a key aspect of "Anglican identity" to embrace an acceptable range of diversity in theology, ecclesiology, and practice. And, for good and ill, we have not defined "acceptable diversity" in a way that makes it clear where the boundaries around these topics are, let alone where they ought to be. To put this in its bluntest form: What do Anglicans believe it is *not* acceptable to believe about the presence of Christ in the Eucharist and lay presidency at that sacrament (for example)?

To put it another way, the question for Episcopalians and Anglicans in our official gatherings is not so much "Can I believe what these other Christian believe about (for example) the presence of Christ in the Eucharist?" The question, rather, is "Can I be in communion with other Christians who believe this about the presence of Christ?" And more often than perhaps we are willing to recognize, the answer to this must be "Yes!"—and in no small part because we *already are* in communion with other Christians who believe this:[1] They are Episcopalians, Anglicans; and we need not hold identical beliefs in order to be in communion with each other. Indeed, one of the purposes of the Chicago-Lambeth Quadrilateral is to declare precisely this. We—Anglicans of all sorts and conditions—together affirm these things, and we are not only happy but eager to come into fuller communion with others who do as well. And, by extension, we will find it much more difficult to come into fuller communion with those who don't affirm these things.

---

1 I am most grateful to the Reverend Dr. J. Robert Wright for his clarification of this point as part of the Anglican-Roman Catholic Consultation in the United States (ARCUSA).

The truth of this is borne out in dialogues with Lutherans, Methodists, Presbyterians, Roman Catholics, and many others.

Bishop Gregg is quite right in highlighting the important issues I have summarized above. We do in fact need greater clarity about what we believe, and why we believe it. We do in fact need greater clarity about how theology, ecclesiology, and ecclesial practice are interdependent. We do in fact need greater clarity about how we judge the adequacy of particular positions and practices in relation to "the essentials of the Christian faith," and the criteria for making those judgments.

And there is a special gift accompanying that clarity when it comes through honest, charitable, and deep dialogue with others, perhaps especially dialogue across lines of difference: That dialogue in and of itself increases our real but imperfect communion, even when it does not lead to short- or medium-term publicly visible unity.

At the same time, ecumenical dialogue is not the only place where theological, ecclesiological, and ecclesial clarity develops. Nor is it the case that clarity on all matters must be achieved before churches can move toward visible unity.

Two things need to be said here.

First, not all difference on issues is divisive, and not all divisive issues are, in fact, church-dividing. Anglicans and Episcopalians recognize the truth of this even in the midst of ongoing disputes, disagreements, and divisions with our own church and within the Anglican Communion. We do not find it necessary to have complete clarity, identical language, or uniform practice in order to be in communion with each other. We do not even need to pray the same prayers in the same language.

Generally speaking, church-dividing issues are those that are doctrinal: They call into question whether a church may see that the other holds "the essentials of the Christian Faith."[2] Differences on central doctrine are expressed variously, including in difference of theology and practice in areas such as the nature of the Supper of the Lord/ the Holy Eucharist, the exercise of authority, ordained ministry, and so on. One of the tasks of ecumenical dialogue is to discern the extent to which what has divided churches in the past need continue to be church-dividing. So, for example, there are among churches quite different ways of speaking about God, the person and work of Christ, the mission of God and of the church, Holy Baptism, and so on. Yet in many cases, churches have been able, by the grace of God, to see

---

2 "A Theological Foundation."

through notable differences to a mutual recognition that other churches
hold "the essentials of the Christian Faith."

"A Theological Foundation" makes it clear that the Episcopal Church
and the United Methodist Church do in fact recognize in each other
the essentials of the Christian Faith: It is a fact that "Anglicans and
Methodists, and specifically the predecessor churches of the Episcopal
Church and the United Methodist Church, have not, *as churches*, called
into question the faith, the ministerial orders, or the sacraments of the
other church."[3] This is a very precise and important statement. It indicates that while our churches are divided, those divisions are not in and
of themselves church-dividing. That is, our divisions do not point to
fundamental, irreconcilable differences concerning "the essentials of the
Christian Faith."[4] Further, the statement indicates that while individuals
and even groups within each church may in good faith and conscience
call into question particular beliefs and practices, the church *as such*—
that is, formally and authoritatively as a duly constituted body—has not
done so and does not do so now.

In the first sentence of the section "Issues Perceived as Separating
Our Churches" the statement is made that "there are some areas of
church life and teachings that are. . . church dividing issues." Nowhere,
however, does "A Theological Foundation" indicate what precisely these
issues are or the basis on which they actually are church-dividing and
legitimately so. The rest of the document runs quite against this single
sentence. It seems to me, then, both wise and charitable to consider this
sentence ill-phrased rather than an assertion of established fact.

Further, "A Theological Foundation" states in concise but comprehensive ways the key (or essential) elements of the Christian faith that
the two churches affirm together.[5] And in the subsections of "Issues
Perceived as Separating Our Churches," the document lays out in more
detail where the two churches already affirm common beliefs, even while
going on to explore some indications that differences remain that may
be *perceived* as church-dividing. Some of these issues have already been
resolved within one or both of the two churches in ways that remove
the legitimate basis of the perception of division. (See, for example, the
section on Baptism and regeneration.) Other issues—such as the presence of Christ in Holy Communion—may appear to be deeply divisive,
but when one looks more closely and at current official documents, it
becomes clear that these differences are matters of emphasis, and in any

---

3 "A Theological Foundation," 8; emphasis added.
4 "A Theological Foundation."
5 "A Theological Foundation," 14.

case exist as much within each church as between the two. Yet other issues—race and class particularly—are identified as historical rather than doctrinal. They affect both churches, and one of the gifts of fuller communion, it is to be hoped, is increased ability and willingness to address these issues more effectively by addressing them together.

From this angle, then, "A Theological Foundation" makes these basic and necessary claims:

- There is good and ample reason to recognize that the Episcopal Church and the United Methodist Church separately and together hold the essentials of the Christian faith.

- Though the churches are, in fact, divided, this is not necessary in order to preserve either church's witness to the Christian faith. Differences that might in the past perhaps have risen to this significance have been resolved.

- Current significant differences are of one or both of two types: acceptable diversity within either or both churches; and/or differences that arise from factors that both churches individually have determined must be overcome, and may be best overcome together.

Does "A Theological Foundation" itself give a completely adequate and satisfying account of why all this is the case? No. But it does not have to. And that is my second point.

Ecumenical documents that state agreements or commonalities do so in summary form. They do not claim to adduce all the evidence necessary to do so. It's generally accepted that we need not explicate in detail that upon which we already agree. Doing so may underscore the point that we already agree on much more than we disagree about. And "A Theological Foundation" summarizes the broad, crucial agreement in the section "Affirmations."[6]

Further, documents that deal with divisive issues and reach the kind of conclusion outlined above depend on long, careful, well-informed, critically examined study and argumentation that takes place during the course of a particular dialogue over many years. In some cases, this dialogue has taken place in other ways that can bear scrutiny, often because such discussions have led to a greater degree of visible communion.

And it is a general methodological principle of ecumenical dialogues that where two churches have worked out a way forward on divisive

6 "A Theological Foundation," 14–15.

issues such that a greater degree of visible unity is possible—as is the case with the Episcopal Church and the Evangelical Lutheran Church in America, for example—it is not necessary to reproduce the same argument a second, third, or fourth time when the same issue is present between other churches—as, here, between the Episcopal Church and the United Methodist Church.

Quite concretely: If TEC and ELCA have reached substantial, formal, recognized agreement on the historic episcopate, and the ELCA and the UMC hold substantively similar (if not identical) views on the historic episcopate, it is not necessary to reargue the matter from the beginning in dialogue between TEC and the UMC.

Note that this is not the same as saying "the partner of my partner is therefore automatically also my partner." The fact that the ELCA is in full communion with both TEC and the UMC does not thereby put TEC and UMC into full communion. Rather, it suggests that what has been achieved by one dialogue—for example, in the process leading up to full communion between TEC and the ELCA—may very well provide the kind of work needed in another one. There's no need to reinvent the wheel when the existing wheel has been deemed to be what is needed.

Even so: It is well worth noting that "A Theological Foundation" does not do some clearly necessary things, including proposing a way forward that will make visible fuller communion between the Episcopal Church and the United Methodist Church. But, again, it does not need to. The purposes of "A Theological Foundation" are different. It is, explicitly, a document that expresses the views of the members of an officially constituted dialogue at a particular point in time. It is not a formally authorized statement of agreement between the two churches. That being said, it clearly leads in the direction of a formally authorized statement by summarizing the fruits of the dialogue thus far and indicating that, in the opinion of the dialogue participants, no further doctrinal work is necessary before the two churches can consider moving into more visible unity. And in this way "A Theological Foundation" is of great significance. It may not be sufficient in itself, but then, it doesn't claim to be.

So what remains to be done to move TEC and the UMC into fuller visible unity? The answer to this question depends to considerable extent on what judgment one makes about the claims of "A Theological Foundation." And here a particular problem arises that is not discussed explicitly in "A Theological Foundation" yet is suggested by Bishop Gregg's response: the problem of adequacy of evidence. Put bluntly, how do we know with an adequate degree of likelihood that Episcopalians and Methodists do in fact believe what they say they believe? In part, this is a matter of presentation of existing evidence—and that "A Theological Foundation" does do in many ways. But it is also a matter of whether the existing evidence is itself sufficiently robust and substantial to be convincing.

This is a familiar question in the ecumenical dialogues in which the Episcopal Church and the Anglican Communion are engaged. Anglicans do not have a clear, elaborated body of belief expressed as authoritative doctrine (as, for example, the Roman Catholic Church does). Nor do we have authoritative confessional statements (as do the Lutherans and the Presbyterians). Nor do we have a commonly accepted magisterial theologian whose theological positions guide us (such as Martin Luther or John Calvin). What we have is common worship, and what we have is an embodied and quite rich tradition of theology, spirituality, and practice. But by their very nature, these things do not provide single definitive statements that can be cited. Both sorts of evidence require extensive interpretation to disclose their import, yet the frames of interpretation are various and changeable depending on time and context. And this poses a challenge in authenticating our claims in ways that are clearly recognizable by and acceptable to others.

It's worth noting that the Wesleyan/Methodist tradition is in a quite similar situation. We are, after all, members of the same family.

In practice, particularly in this dialogue, this means each dialogue partner must do two things: muster the best evidence and best argument available; and, more difficult, trust that our dialogue partner is doing the same thing. Trust is something that is both earned and granted, and the mustering of evidence and argument contributes to earning trust. But it is also necessary to undertake the hard work of developing habits and dispositions that tend toward understanding and trust rather than toward suspicion. And this is no easy work. It is work that is accomplished in actual, concrete, sustained practice at least as much as it is in inward development. The practice of trust is always the practice of risk. And here we are talking about the organizational practice of trust. Quite concretely, we are faced with the work of trusting others even when their statements and practices are susceptible to multiple interpretations—as are ours.

The organizational form of the question about communion that I posed earlier is not "Can (or do) we as a church believe what these others say they believe?" but "Can we as a church be in communion with people who believe these things?" Can the Episcopal Church be in communion with the United Methodist Church, which has said and done particular things?

My own judgment here is that we can, because we are already in communion with people who believe these things and are Episcopalians and Anglicans. The theological affirmations, ecclesiological positions, and ecclesial practices of the United Methodist Church are all readily found already in the Episcopal Church.

For those who make this judgment, there is no legitimate reason to require greater clarity or agreement from this dialogue partner than the Episcopal Church requires within itself. We cannot justly and fairly require more of our partners than we require of ourselves.

And if the Episcopal Church is not willing to break communion within itself in these areas, there is no legitimate theological or ecclesiological reason for not moving toward fuller communion with the United Methodist Church. The questions that remain are how? And when?

The Reverend Ellen K. Wondra, PhD, is Professor of Theology and Ethics in the Bexley Hall Seabury Western Theological Seminary Foundation, and Academic Dean for the Seabury site.

CHAPTER 7

Reflections on Race, Sexuality, and Other Threats to Potential Unity

C. Franklin Brookhart

This essay seeks to address the following sections of "A Theological Foundation" document:

3.8 Issues of Internal Denominational Unity that May Hinder Full Communion

3.9 Experiences of Race/Racism in the Histories of our Churches

3.10 Teaching and Practices related to Human Sexuality

3.11 Issues related to the National Origins of Our Churches and the Growing International Character of Our Churches Today.

I will address each section briefly and conclude with some remarks about ways forward toward a full communion relationship.

Section 3.8 highlights internal threats, tensions of schism, and sub-communities that may hinder full communion. As always, these are issues of power and turf, and beneath these factors the document wisely comments that the basic question is "who really owns this church?"

The problem—some might even call it sin—is that these threats distract from our common proclamation of the Good News of Jesus Christ and from the common mission and ministry we together carry out in the Risen One's name. Both denominations have stories about how conflict eats up much of the available energy in the church at all levels of its life.

These tensions, of course, take on institutional aspects, but the issues are much deeper, and, therefore, require a more profound analysis about our identity in Christ and the emotional, intellectual, and theological assumptions we make which stand in the way of living out our Baptisms.

Section 3.9 seeks to address the persistent, delicate, and deeply rooted sin of racism. This topic has been squarely on the table in all the meetings of the dialogue team from the beginning of the discussions. The dialogue team itself is composed of both African American and European American members. Several of our meetings were given over exclusively to the issues of racism in our histories and lives today. The first took place in March, 2007, in Atlanta, when we met at the Interdenominational Theological Center, a consortium of six predominately African American seminaries. We met in small groups, worshipped in the chapel with the community, and had ecclesiological discussions with faculty and students. Most of us left discouraged about the scars and depth of pain left by the racism of both of our churches. At another meeting in 2008 at Southern Methodist University we had papers presented by black scholars describing and analyzing the experience of African Americans in both of our churches. Finally, we met with a large group of pastors from the historic African American Methodist churches in Chicago. Again, it was a serious meeting, but we left with a sense that some issues had, at least, been clarified, if not resolved, and we pressed these leaders to be part of the future meetings of the dialogue team, an invitation that has yet to yield fruit.

We members of the dialogue team recognize that our churches have not lived out the fullness, the catholicity, of the Gospel. But our meetings have been, I believe, a model for the future of our churches. We did the sometimes painful work of meeting at length, listening to each other's stories and understanding, responding, asking for forgiveness and praying together. The way forward means carrying on in larger contexts this often arduous work while enveloping ourselves in prayer to the One who breaks down all barriers.

Section 3.10 of "A Theological Foundation" raises another issue that has threatened the unity of both of our churches and that could be a deal-breaker for our dialogue. This is, of course, the issue of human sexuality, especially the place of gay and lesbian people in the church. In our discussion it became quickly clear that each church has groups that hold opposing yet strongly felt and carefully argued positions; this tension manifested itself in the meeting of the dialogue team itself. We also know that neither this bilateral dialogue nor our possible future together as full communion partners is going to resolve this situation quickly or easily.

Given this stress both between and among members of our churches, note that the document clearly states that each church's internal policies and standards for ordination will continue to be in force and practice. That is, any interchange of clergy in a full communion arrangement will unfold according to the discipline and canons of the church receiving the cleric.

Since the writing and distribution of "A Theological Foundation," the Episcopal Church has, at its 2012 General Convention, authorized the use of a liturgical resource until the next General Convention in 2015. The rite, entitled "The Witnessing and Blessing of a Lifelong Covenant," is accompanied by extensive resources by which dioceses, congregations, and individuals can learn together and discuss these complex issues. Note that the term "gay marriage" is avoided; this rite is not a marriage ceremony, but is exactly what it calls itself, a liturgy for witnessing and blessing a couple who have made vows of lifelong fidelity. No priest or congregation can be forced to use it or punished for not using it. While this ceremony may be of interest to some United Methodists it is not authorized for use in that church.

Both of our churches live as part of the mainstream of American life, and we are both caught in the far-reaching and rapid societal changes regarding gay and lesbian people. We both seek to remain faithful and relevant churches in the midst of this turmoil. One of the advantages of a full communion arrangement would be that we are working on this together; it could be a gift that we give each other if we were to be involved in discussing this moral issue. Our theological faculties and bishops especially could move forward productively as they work together to discern the Lord's will for the church. Again, full communion relationship will not easily resolve these issues, but it would surely enrich the churches in their discernment of God's will.

Section 3.11 notes both churches were formed in the early days of the American republic and both have origins in the United Kingdom. Over the intervening years, however, both have increasingly come to be composed of people from many places and all races. Further, both are international bodies. The Episcopal Church can be found in seventeen nations in North, Central and South America, in the Pacific region, Africa and Europe. The United Methodist Church is similarly extended around the world. But each church works with this situation in its own way. The Episcopal Church's highest authority is the General Convention, in which all bishops and dioceses from around the world are represented. The highest legislative body of the United Methodist Church is its General Conference, made up of lay and clergy delegates elected from each conference of the denomination worldwide. Central Conferences (outside the United States) also gather quadrennially to adapt legislation made by the General Conference or create additional legislation (both within some limits) needed for their particular contexts. Unlike the Episcopal Church, the role of bishops in these legislative assemblies is solely to preside during plenary sessions. They have neither voice nor vote on any matter presented before the body. Finally, both churches are part of world-wide bodies: the Anglican Communion and the World Methodist Conference respectively. Again, we both live in a diverse and shrinking world that challenges us in our mission and ministry. Yet nothing in this complex picture represents an obstacle to full communion.

Allow me to make four concluding comments. First, to live together in a full communion arrangement does not mean that we are merging or that we agree on all issues. Indeed, both churches have trouble agreeing among themselves on certain topics, yet manage to live together.

Second, what full communion does ask of us is that we recognize each other to be a part of the one, holy, catholic, and apostolic church. We can see the other as a full and legitimate part of the same family, not that we are theological, liturgical, or spiritual clones of each other. Can we agree on the basics enough to trust each other in a future lived together in a closer and more cooperative relationship?

Third, a full communion arrangement, while recognizing places of disagreement, does insist that we learn to live more closely together in the future. It asks that we talk, that we pray for each other, that we study together, and that, when appropriate, we minister together. "A Theological Foundation" shows that we share enough in common so that we can join hands and walk with and to the Risen Christ.

Finally, full communion may well be a way that we both can bear more good fruit for the Kingdom. For much of the New Testament, for instance, the bottom-line test of one's discipleship is if there are fruits of the Holy Spirit present and active. Do we not clearly see an abundance of fruit in each other? Is it not possible that cross-pollination could help us grow more fruit? Would it not be a shame to step aside from this God-given opportunity?

C. Franklin Brookhart is Bishop
of the Diocese of Montana, The Episcopal Church.

CHAPTER 8

Episcopalians, United Methodists, and the Historic Episcopate

William B. Oden

The bilateral dialogue between the Episcopal Church and the United Methodist church has reached the point where both communions have affirmed "Interim Shared Eucharist." We are now in a time of getting to know each other with a period of mutual reception, bishop-to-bishop, pastor-to-pastor, and congregation-to-congregation. It is a time of sharing worship, mission, and ever-deepening mutual understanding.

The Goal and Nature of Full Communion

The goal is full communion in faith, order, and mission. The term "full communion" grew out of numerous ecumenical dialogues, and is one expression of the unity of the church prayed for by Jesus. A consensus of the nature of full communion has emerged through these dialogues, including "Make Us One in Christ," a foundational statement of TEC/UMC dialogue. In essence, full communion is a living relationship between distinct churches, recognizing each other as catholic and apostolic churches, holding the essentials of the Christian faith whereby the reconciliation, recognition of apostolicity of clergy orders, interchangeability of ordained ministers, and shared Eucharist is then fully possible.

Full communion is not the same as organic union or merger, but is widely recognized as a significant step toward the full visible unity of all Christians. The bilateral dialogue (see Article VI, UMC Constitution) between the Episcopal Church and the United Methodist Church has reached agreement on the ingredients necessary for a relationship of full communion. In "Make Us One in Christ," the foundation of our dialogue, the following requirements for full communion have been met:

- Both churches affirm the primacy of scripture as containing the Word of God.

- Both churches affirm that each belongs to the one, holy, catholic, and apostolic church.

- Both churches affirm the Apostles' and Nicene Creed as full expressions of Trinitarian faith.

- Both churches affirm the two sacraments, Baptism and the Eucharist, as instituted by Jesus and as rightly administered by ordained clergy.

- Both churches affirm that personal and corporate oversight (*episkopé*) is embodied and exercised as a visible expression of apostolic ministry.

- Both churches affirm the threefold ministry of bishop, presbyter, and deacon.

And here is the rub: the Episcopal Church, as a part of the Anglican Communion, is committed to the Chicago-Lambeth Quadrilateral,[1] containing the four elements necessary for unity, though not essential for salvation. These four are:

1. Primacy of scripture, both the Old and New Testaments;

2. The Apostles' and Nicene Creeds;

3. Two sacraments, Baptism and Eucharist, rightly administered;

4. And the historic episcopate, "locally adapted in the methods of its administration to the varying needs of the nations and peoples called of God into the Unity of His Church."[2]

The Historic Episcopate

The fourth is the one obstacle to overcome for the United Methodist Church: the receiving of the historic episcopate. According to Episcopal historian Dr. J. Robert Wright, the Episcopal Church has no formal definition of the historic episcopate except the one hammered out in the Episcopal Church-Evangelical Lutheran Church of America dialogue:

---

1 John A. Bross, *John Wesley's Ordinations for America in 1784 Calmly Reconsidered: Perspectives for the Future of Episcopal-United Methodist Relations* (Evanston, IL: Seabury Western Theological Seminary, 2004), 66–67.
2 Bross, 67.

The historic episcopate is one important strand in the apostolicity of the church. It is a sign of the church's intention to remain faithful to the apostolic teaching and mission of the gospel, at the same time that it is also a sign of the final ingathering of all of God's humanity foretold in Matthew 19:28. It is a succession of bishops or church leaders whose roots are planted in the time of the early church, pointing back to the centrality of Christ and the teaching of the apostles, and to such other strands of apostolicity as the biblical canon, the creeds and councils, and the sacraments, while at the same time pointing forward in order to oversee, or superintend, or give leadership to, the mission of the church today. . . [It] is 'a sign though not a guarantee,' in personal terms, of the unity and continuity of the church's faith throughout time and space.[3]

The historic episcopate—called "apostolic succession" in Wesley's day—was a major issue in the two churches' beginnings. In America at the conclusion of the Revolutionary War, there were three branches of the Anglican Church: the New England Anglicans led by Samuel Seabury, a Pennsylvania group led by William White, and the Methodists (not yet separated from the Church of England) led by Frances Asbury. From the beginning, America had no Church of England bishop. The bishop of London, who was responsible for the North American mission field, refused to ordain a Methodist bishop or one for the other two branches. Any Church of England bishop had to pledge loyalty to the crown. Understandably, many Anglican clergy left for England or Canada following the war, leaving flocks without shepherds. According to Wesley historian Gareth Lloyd,

[Wesley's] ordinations were a direct result of the establishment of an independent United States. The position of the Anglican Church, which in any case had never been as dominant as in the mother country, was severely damaged by the independence struggle. In Virginia for example, only 28 clergymen remained out of a pre-war total of 98 and services had been discontinued in almost half of the Anglican churches. It was virtually impossible in such a chaotic situation for Methodists to have easy sacramental access and this had been the

case even before the War as the Church struggled to cope
with a frontier society.

John Wesley's dilemma was that ordination of itinerants
appeared the only viable solution. Yet this would signify
formal separation from the Anglican Church by allowing lay
preachers to perform the sacraments. Wesley would therefore
expose himself to the charge of inconsistency with regard
to this often professed and controversial claim of Anglican
allegiance. His brother Charles underlined this fact in the
immediate aftermath of the ordinations when he obtained
the opinion of Lord Chief Justice Mansfield, one of Britain's
highest ranking legal authorities, to the effect that "Ordination was Separation."[4]

John Wesley had moved from high church to latitudinarianism[5]
in his ecclesiology. Following the Richard Hooker, Bishop Edward
Stillingfleet, and Lord Peter King understanding of church orders,
Wesley had come to the position that bishops and presbyters (elders) were
of the same order and, following the example of the Alexandrian church
in the Patristic era, bishops could be chosen and ordained by presbyters
in emergency situations when no ordained bishop was available.

John Bross, an Episcopal lay theologian, has written a significant study
of Wesley's ordinations.[6] He traced two streams of apostolic succession.
One, the high church position, envisioned a "power line" going back to
the apostles and "hand to head" unbroken in the history of the church.
Validity of orders depended upon participation in the unbroken power
line. This position was also defended half a century after Wesley by the
Oxford renewal movement, including Newman and the Tractarians.

The second stream, that of the latitudinarians, following Hooker,
interpreted apostolic succession with more flexibility, while affirming it
began in "apostolic times" and saw it as a significant symbol of the continuity of the faithfulness of the ministry of the church.

According to Bross, the Tractarian view prevailed until the latter part
of the twentieth century when the Episcopal Church's involvement in

4 Gareth Lloyd, "The Response of British Methodists to John Wesley's Ordinations to North
America." Paper delivered during the Wesley in America Conference, Perkins School of
Theology, Dallas, TX, April 3–5, 2003.
5 Latitudinarian is defined as "any group of Anglican churchmen of the 17th century who
favored freedom of belief and was opposed to varying forms of worship or doctrine."
[Webster's New Twentieth Century Dictionary of the English Language, Unabridged
(New York; Simon & Schuster, c1983)]
6 Bross, 67.

ecumenical dialogues (especially the ELCA) called for an understanding of the historic episcopate as closer to Hooker's.[7]

In light of this abbreviated history, let us look closely at Wesley's American ordinations:

1. A pastoral crisis was growing ever more severe. Few ordained clergy were available to administer the sacraments.

2. All three Church of England related groups—the New England Anglicans, the White element, and the Methodists—sought solutions.

3. Wesley had arrived at the conclusion that emergency situations allowed for irregular ordinations.

4. When all attempts to have a bishop ordained for American Methodists failed, Wesley, as a "scriptural *episkopos*," ordained Thomas Coke a general superintendent on September 1 and 2, 1784, and sent him to America to ordain Francis Asbury as co-general superintendent to lead the American Methodists. Wesley also ordained Richard Whatcoat and Thomas Vasey as elders to accompany Coke to America to give leadership to the American Methodists.

5. While Wesley clearly did not see these ordinations as separation from the Church of England, others (including his brother Charles) did understand Wesley's activity to be precisely that.

6. Seabury finally attained ordination through the Scottish Episcopal Church, and while the act was also controversial, the Seabury-White factions came together in November 1787, three years after Asbury's ordination, and the Protestant Episcopal Church was born.

7. Thus, we had two Episcopal churches formed in America— one with bishops remaining in the apostolic succession, one with bishops outside of the historic succession. (A Methodist mantra affirms that Asbury was every ounce a true bishop with his saddle as his cathedral.) Despite the break due to Wesley's ordinations, thereafter the Methodists continued an orderly succession.

---

7 Bross, 23.

8. There is neither time nor space to go into depth on the nature of the episcopacy Wesley birthed through his ordination. It should at least be noted that beyond all the confusion and arguments as to how Wesley understood his general superintendency, his action and Asbury's leadership that followed created a unique episcopacy in Christianity:

9. An unbroken line of consecration, once established

10. An itinerant episcopacy—not diocesan

11. Conciliar and corporate before personal

12. Evolving into an episcopacy with global authority by the nineteenth century

Two Separate Paths

The two churches took different paths of mission and direction. From 1784 to 1948, there was little formal contact. The following events brought the churches into bilateral dialogue approved by both communions in 1998:

It really began in 1936 when William Temple, the archbishop of York (later Archbishop of Canterbury), had written that he "could only agree to union or any approval to full 'intercommunion' on the basis of the agreement that all future ordinations are Episcopal. But if that is agreed, I would go far in recognizing the *de facto* efficacy of existing ministries."[8]

The Church of South India was founded upon this principle in 1947. There would be no re-ordinations, but all new bishops of the church were to be consecrated by three bishops in the historic episcopate (the number agreed upon by the Council of Nicaea, 325 CE). All new clergy would be ordained by bishops in the succession.

The Temple statement and the South India United Church motivated the following exploration between the Episcopal Church and the Methodist Church (quoting from the 1948 Episcopal General Convention Journal):

Intercommunion with the Protestant Episcopal Church: the Methodist General Conference of 1948, meeting in Boston, was requested by the Protestant Episcopal Church to create a Commission which could discuss ways and means of achieving

---

8 Bross, 70.

intercommunion and possibly union. In response, the General Conference established a Commission patterned after the Protestant Episcopal commission with eighteen members, six bishops, six clergy and six laymen. Bishop Ivan Lee Holt served as first chairman.[9]

The Blake-Pike Proposal in 1960 called for a united church that was truly catholic, truly reformed, and truly evangelical. Both churches agreed to dispense with their conversations in order to participate in the Consultation on Church Union.

Participation in the World Council of Churches, especially the Faith and Order Commission, which produced the groundbreaking Lima Report, "Baptism, Eucharist, and Ministry." This report affirmed the historic episcopate as a sign, though not a guarantee of apostolicity.[10]

The International Anglican/Methodist dialogue called for by the 1988 Lambeth Conference and 1992 World Methodist Council. The 1996 World Methodist Council approved "Sharing the Apostolic Communion"[11] and the 1998 Lambeth Conference affirmed the report and referred it to the provinces for study.[12] Out of that directive, bilateral dialogues began immediately both in England and America. Both dialogues are nearing their concluding stages, both calling for closer communion between Anglicans and Methodists.

The TEC/UMC dialogue is now at the point of addressing the major barrier toward full communion—the historic episcopate. From a United Methodist perspective the question is clear: What would receiving the historic episcopate mean for United Methodism? In my judgment, there is only one reason not to move forward:

If the "high church" position would be assumed, then in essence the act would be used to validate our invalid orders. Therefore, the act would constitute re-ordination. A recent paper by Professor Geoffrey Wainwright raises the question of whether the historic episcopate is inflexible dogma, or whether there truly is flexibility to share it as a gift.[13]

There are several reasons for the United Methodist Church to accept the "sign" of the historic episcopate:

---

9 "Report by the commission on Church Union," Journal of the General Conference, the Methodist Church, 1964.
10 "Baptism, Eucharist, and Ministry," The Word Council of Churches (Geneva: 1984).
11 Lambeth Conference Resolution no 64; World Methodist Council Resolution XV, 1996.
12 Lambeth Conference Resolution IV. 17, 1998
13 Geoffrey Wainwright, "Is Episcopal Succession a Matter of Dogma for Anglicans: The Evidence of Some Recent Dialogues."

1. Our Book of Discipline calls for the Council of Bishops to lead the church in an ongoing search for unity;[14]

2. The breach that occurred between Methodists and Anglicans in America following the Revolutionary War would be healed;

3. United Methodism would join two-thirds of Christianity in affirming the sign as a symbol of the unity and apostolicity of the church, though not with the same theological perspective;

4. The two churches could then have ministry that would be recognized and reconciled, allowing for interchangeability.

5. In essence, the United Methodist Council of Bishops has already affirmed the historic episcopate by a positive response to the COCU Consensus (which was drafted by Perkins professor John Deshner).[15] However, what was swallowed may not have been digested.

It is important that these issues be squarely faced. In papers presented to the Faith and Order Conference in Kuala Lumpur, 2005, Rowan Williams (Anglican Archbishop of Canterbury) and Stanley Hauerwas (then a United Methodist theologian) had complementary papers calling for more honesty between dialogical partners in dealing with the tough dividing issues.[16]

One tough issue is the manner in which the historic episcopate would be conferred. The United Methodist understanding of *episkope* is conciliar and communal before it is personal. (Thus a bishop is named to the Council of Bishops before being assigned to an Episcopal area.[17]) The model of the Church of South India and the TEC/ELCA model of gradual inclusion of bishops into the historic episcopate would not be feasible. The United Methodist bishops could not accept a "two-tier" episcopacy, but would need to enter as a total Council, either at a national gathering or a national gathering of leadership bishops followed by regional gatherings. The historic episcopate was not totally passed on at either the Church of South India or ELCA celebration of full communion (with all future Episcopal ordinations/consecrations using at least three "hands on" bishops in the succession over a thirty-year

---

14   See Article V of Division One of the Constitution; Also, "Specific Responsibilities of Bishops," para. 414.6, 2401, The Book of Discipline of the United Methodist Church (Nashville, TN: The United Methodist Publishing House, 2012, 137).

15   COCU Consensus (1985), para. 48–51.

16   The Ecumenical Review, Vol.57, No.5, October 2005, 372–81.

17   United Methodist Book of Discipline, para.427.

period). Full communion would then occur after all bishops not sharing in the historic episcopate were dead.

A Way Forward

With the Williams–Hauerwas concerns before us, let us consider a way forward: The ultimate pathway to full communion between the Episcopal Church and the United Methodist Church will be through leadership of the bishops of the two churches, approval by the House of Bishops and the Council of Bishops, and ratification by the United Methodist General Conference and the Episcopal General Convention.

The following is only a premature and very tentative beginning model from a United Methodist perspective. The actual process has no specific timeline or limits. These will be determined by reception of the proposed agreement by local churches, dioceses, and annual conferences.

According to "Make Us One With Christ: The Study Guide Version," recognizing each other's ministries will pave the road to full communion.

By its formal approval of "the COCU Consensus" in 1988, the United Methodist Church signaled its willingness to understand the episcopacy as a third order of ministry while retaining it as an office, and indicated its desire to incorporate historic episcopal succession as a visible sign of apostolic continuity.

The manner of the reconciliation of the two episcopacies is still a matter of discussion and study. As part of this discussion, it is our hope that with regard to a future reconciliation of ministries, Episcopalians and United Methodists will affirm the following:

1. Our journey toward full communion will include a way to recognize and reconcile the two episcopacies in such a manner as not to call into question the authenticity of each other's ordinations;

2. Both churches affirm the historic episcopate, in the language of the "Baptism, Eucharist and Ministry" statement as a "sign, but not a guarantee, of the catholicity, unity, and continuity of the church;"

3. Both churches agree that the historic episcopate is always in a process of reform in the service of the Gospel;

4. From their formative periods in the colonial age both churches locally adapted the historic episcopate for the sake of mission.

With the above foundational statement, the following process is suggested: The appointment of a task force composing at least three bishops from each church, including the two dialogue chairs, and liturgical theologians from each church to create a resolution with the necessary canonical and disciplinary provisions to be presented to both bodies of bishops, and the drafting of a liturgical celebration of full communion that would include the sharing of mutual gifts. A major issue would be the question of liturgical choreography.

As in the Church of South India celebration, it would be expected that God would bless the two churches with the gift of "fuller communion, while remaining two distinct churches."[18] Remaining to be resolved is the manner in which the "sign" of the historic episcopate would be offered. While the Porvoo Agreement (1990) cannot be used as a model, there are several similarities to the Methodist historical situation. Nordic and Baltic Lutheran churches, during the Protestant Reformation, broke the historic succession by having bishops ordained by priests who were deans of cathedrals because no Anglican bishops were available due to the political situation. The Irish and British Anglican churches, after years of dialogue, concluded that it was the "intention" of these Lutheran churches to be faithful to apostolicity with no further liturgical action required. It is not being suggested that the situations are parallel, only that the break in the succession does not have to be unresolvable.

The issue for United Methodists is what physical sign (along with prayers) would be used to be certain there would be no semblance to re-ordination, e.g. hands on heads, on shoulders, handshakes.

It must be emphasized that there should be no rush to completion of the process toward full communion. The Holy Spirit does not always conform to human and institutional schedules. The above should be seen only as a way to begin conversations concerning a way forward.

The House of Bishops of the Church of England, in a paper entitled "Apostolicity and Succession" stated:

---

18 The consultation, held in August 2005, included Dan Benedict (Director, Section on Worship, The Board of Discipleship), Professor Mark Stamm (Perkins School of Theology), Professor Diedra Kriewald (Wesley School of Theology), Bishop William B. Oden, and two staff members of GCCUIC, the Reverand Betty Gamble and Dr. Doug Mills. The writer of this paper would also like to express appreciation to colleagues Jim Kirby and Ted Campbell of Perkins School of Theology and Russell E. Richey of Candler School of Theology for their willingness to read and decipher a very rough paper. Also thanks to Michelle Morris and Tom Giusti for many hours of decoding impossible scribble.

Otherwise apparently promising schemes have foundered on the rock of the "historic episcopal succession" and the "reconciliation of ministries." In recent years, however, fresh ways of approaching this question [the historic episcopate] have been discovered in a number of ecumenical dialogues, which have in consequence begun to show convergence on this issue. In some areas this convergence is resulting in a consensus. Representatives of different traditions have come to recognize on the one hand that the apostolicity of the Church is wider than the historic Episcopal succession and on the other hand that integral to the ministry of oversight is the service of helping to maintain the Church in the faith of the apostles and that orderly continuity in the ministry of oversight (*episcope*) is one of the means given by God for maintaining the Church in the faith of the apostles.[19]

The report concludes that "convergences in theological dialogues, like those with . . . the Methodists, suggest that even seemingly intractable questions may find resolution if we are faithful to our calling and open to receive God's gift of unity."[20]

Let us pray without ceasing the Eucharistic Prayer of both churches, "By your Spirit, make us one in Christ, one with each other, and one in ministry to all the world."

William Oden is a retired bishop in the United Methodist connection and served as Co-Chair for the Episcopal-United Methodist Dialogue Team.

---

19 "Apostolicity and Succession," House of Bishops Occasional Paper (The Church of England, 1994), 3.

20 "Apostolicity and Succession," 34.

CHAPTER 9

"Duncan, Why Don't We . . . "

Duncan Gray

I belong to a very special small group of bishops—Roman Catholic, United Methodist, and Episcopal—whose predecessors forged a special relationship during the turbulent years of the 1950s and 1960s in Mississippi. Together those bishops found support with one another, planned together the various ways that they collectively could be instruments of healing and hope in a tragic time, and initiated a wide variety of common ministries of advocacy through the years. Standing on the shoulders of those significant colleagues of years ago, the bishops of these three churches continue to meet regularly at breakfast for mutual fellowship and to search for ways that we can, collectively, address the challenges of education, immigration reform, and other contemporary issues.

It was in the context of this relationship of mutual trust, built on decades of common ministry, that the Interim Eucharistic Sharing agreement adopted in 2006 came into our lives. While our Roman Catholic colleague listened in and added comments from time to time from his unique perspective, the United Methodist bishop, Hope Morgan Ward, and I began to dream about how we might incorporate this agreement in tangible and iconic ways in Mississippi.

We began with the most visible means of marking this new relationship—sharing the Eucharist in each other's most visible venues—our Diocesan Council (convention) and the Annual Mississippi Conference of the United Methodist Church. In both venues during that first year the visiting bishop preached and the host bishop's eucharistic liturgy was used.

At the first Annual Conference, I tried to respond to some of the very real concerns being voiced by United Methodists about all that was going on in the Episcopal Church. I named their concern early on: "When United Methodists hear of this agreement, the first thing many of them say is 'Why do we want to get involved with a church that is being so torn apart by its own internal conflicts?' When Episcopalians hear of this agreement the first thing many of them say is 'Grape juice?'"

Years later, those lines are still quoted back to me when we gather with the United Methodists.

Our conversation began to deepen as Bishop Ward and I searched for ways to incarnate this new sacramental relationship in ever more visible and practical ways. In a conversation with the clergy of our two churches' largest downtown congregations—Galloway United Methodist and St. Andrew's Cathedral—Bishop Ward and I commissioned my ecumenical officer, the Reverend Michael Nations, to draw up an agreement that could become the working guidelines for our common life together in Mississippi. After a variety of modifications were made to the document, we held a major celebration in downtown Jackson on March 3, 2009, the feast day of John and Charles Wesley, to publicly commit to the principles articulated in the document.

We gathered at Galloway UMC for fellowship and dinner and talked about our common history and the work of the Holy Spirit in bringing us to this point. Following dinner, with acolytes bearing crosses and banners and symbols of both churches, we processed the two blocks from Galloway to St. Andrew's for a eucharistic celebration and the formal signing of "A Covenant for Common Life Between the Episcopal Diocese of Mississippi and the United Methodist Conference of Mississippi." (see p. 103) It was an extraordinary moment and continues to warm my heart at its remembrance.

Several actions flowed out of that document. Building on the joy of that moment a decision was made by Bishop Ward and me to celebrate this new relationship with a joint eucharistic celebration on or around March 3 of each year. The event would be co-hosted by one Episcopal and one United Methodist congregation in towns throughout the state. These two congregations would plan the liturgy and other festivities surrounding the event. The "visiting" bishop would preach and the "host" bishop would be the lead celebrant, but everything else would be left to the planning of the local churches. To date (2013), these joint celebrations have taken place in Meridian, Oxford, Natchez, and Gulfport with one scheduled for Clarksdale in 2014. The relationship between these local hosting congregations has deepened and several continue the March 3 celebration even without bishops. Enthusiasm for such occasions has spread, and we are getting more local requests than can be easily accommodated. What a wonderful problem to have! In addition, a significant number of congregations have begun their own joint celebrations with or without bishops in attendance. Even more numerous are the many other ways that local congregations have found to partner with each other across denominational lines in common ministry and mission. The encouragement from their bishops through these very visible and high-profile events have greatly energized their efforts.

Consistent with the Covenant, our diocesan staff and the conference staff of the United Methodist Church met together to study the resource *Make Us One With Christ.* A number of local congregations have been through the entire six-week study, often with United Methodist partners. That study has enriched the relationship immeasurably.

One of the most touching moments for me during my visitations is to hear prayers for Hope (now James) in the same breath as prayers for Rowan (now Justin), Katharine, and Duncan. Not every congregation does it, but enough do to make it extraordinary meaningful.

As our relationship deepened we searched for ways to make this increasingly real to the average person in the pew in ways that were recognizable and practical. Truth be known, it was at this moment that the personalities of our two denominational cultures began to become clearly seen as we struggled to be faithful to our different traditions. More than a few times Bishop Ward would approach me with a particular initiative that was creative, but seemed to me a bit beyond the scope of the boundaries of the eucharistic agreement.

I'd get a phone call: "Duncan, why don't we . . . ?" Consistent with my Anglican establishment traditions, I would often hear myself saying, "Hope, we can't do that." And in true Wesleyan fashion, she would respond, "Why not?" So we would go to work to see if or how we could make something work.

It was in one such phone call that we began to explore joint appointments for clergy in small Mississippi towns. Though the eucharistic celebration would be problematic, the other work of clergy—pastoral care, education, church administration, non-eucharistic worship leadership—could be done, congregation-willing, through a series of negotiated agreements that made expectations very clear about what could be expected of the clergy and congregation.

Today, in the small town of Port Gibson, in southwest Mississippi, you can stand on the side walk of the main street in town facing west toward St. James' Episcopal Church. On the church sign it says, "The Rev. Margaret Ayers, Rector." You can then look east, directly across the street at the Port Gibson United Methodist Church. On its sign reads, "The Rev. Margaret Ayers, Pastor." This Episcopal priest serves both congregations, attends the Annual Mississippi Conference and Diocesan Council, meets with me for her "annual consultation" and consults with "her" district superintendent. It was hard, and sometimes tedious work, but we got it done.

Bishop Ward finished her eight-year assignment last year and the building of trust with my new colleague, Bishop James Swanson, has just begun. It is that trust that allows us to take risks in this new relationship as we seek to understand the gifts of our two traditions that point us to a more full embrace of the gospel. I have no doubt this is the work of the Holy Spirit.

At her last Annual Conference in 2012, Bishop Ward invited me to join her in laying hands on those she would be ordaining as new elders in the United Methodist Church. "Hope, I can't do that," I said.

"Why not?" she responded.

Duncan Gray is Bishop of the Diocese of Mississippi.

A Covenant for Common Life
Between
The Episcopal Diocese of Mississippi And
The United Methodist Conference of Mississippi

PREAMBLE

Be it known by these presents, that we Duncan Montgomery Gray III by Divine Providence, the Episcopal Bishop of Mississippi, and we Hope Morgan Ward, by Divine Providence the United Methodist Bishop of Mississippi desiring to foster the development of common Christian life between our two churches did under the protection of Almighty God on the Feast of John and Charles Wesley, 3 March 2009 in Jackson enter into this solemn agreement to mark a right beginning of our two churches sharing a common mission and a common ministry.

Article 1

We ask that in those cities and towns where our two churches co-exist that the congregations in those places reach out to each other and form partnerships. We desire that these partnerships be established by the end of 2009.

Article 2

We look forward to the day when our national churches are reconciled and brought into full communion with one another. Until that time we commit ourselves to having one shared Eucharist a year in Jackson. We give our permission and blessing for partner congregations to do the same. We require that the *guidelines for such Eucharistic services* be those approved by our national churches in September 2006.

Article 3

We ask the members of our congregations in the course of 12 months to attend Sunday worship in an Episcopal congregation and to attend the Sunday worship in an United Methodist congregation, with members and clergy of the guest congregation being invited to preach, read scripture and offer prayers.

Article 4

We ask our congregations to complete the six week study *Make Us One with Christ* as we commit to complete this study together. We desire that this study be completed no later than 24 months of the establishment of this partnership.

Article 5

We give profound thanks that for many years our congregations have had joint programming and we strongly desire that this joint programming increase and deepen to the greatest extent possible. This programming should include religious education, mission, evangelism, social action, and the joint use of facilities.

Article 6

We commit to continuing the tradition of our predecessors by meeting together monthly to nourish the bonds of fellowship and cooperation. We ask that our clergy follow our example and meet together on a regular basis and to exchange newsletters and other appropriate communications.

Article 7

We ask our congregations to include the names of both Bishops and Congregational Partner Pastors whenever prayers are offered in Sunday worship.

Article 8

This agreement remains in effect until our successors in office are elected or until such time our national churches commit to enter into full communion.

Article 9

We delegate to our Ecumenical Officers to oversee the implementation of this agreement.

In testimony whereof we have affixed our signatures and seal.

_____   _____

CHAPTER 10

Common Life in Mississippi, 2009–2012: An Emerging Vision

Hope Morgan Ward

Episcopalians and United Methodists have been colleague communities and partners in mission in Mississippi for many years, bonding in particular ways during the Civil Rights Movement of the 1960s. The two judicatories have forged an ongoing tradition of communication and partnership, including monthly breakfasts in which the bishops of the two judicatories lived in communication and connection with each other.

A conversation emerged in Mississippi as the Episcopal Church and the United Methodist Church moved forward toward Interim Eucharistic Sharing. Bishop Duncan Gray, Jr., and I convened a small task group of Episcopal and United Methodist leaders to think about forging a "Covenant of Life" between our two churches.

The "Covenant of Life" was drafted, discussed and edited in the community of this small task group. The Covenant of Life included an annual service of preaching and Eucharist led by the Episcopal and United Methodist bishops, a retreat of leaders of our two judicatories for learning more about our respective traditions, regular prayer for the bishops in Sunday worship, and a call for Episcopal and United Methodist churches to partner in local communities for worship, study, prayer, and mission.

Movements into the Covenant

As a first movement into the Covenant, I invited Bishop Gray to preach at the Annual Conference Session in June, 2007, and I invited Episcopalians to be present. Many Episcopal friends were present for this service of worship. The response of the Annual Conference was palpable joy as they welcomed Bishop Gray and Episcopal clergy and laity from their communities.

Bishop Gray invited me to speak at the annual meeting of the diocese in Vicksburg in February, 2009. In these respective ways, we began to embody the principles of the Covenant of Life.

Study: "Make Us One, Lord"

Bishop Gray and I convened a retreat of leaders from our respective judicatories: judicatory staff, significant lay and clergy leaders with an interest in ecumenicity. In preparation, each leader was asked to read the study guide prepared by the Episcopal-United Methodist Dialogue Team. This retreat day offered a time to explore our histories, to note intersections and times of distancing, to speak candidly with one another, and to pose questions.

The retreat was held at Duncan Gray Retreat Center, an Episcopal facility often used by United Methodist groups for retreats and meetings.

The day ended with a service of worship in the chapel of the Gray Center. Participants carried away with them hope for an ongoing Episcopal-United Methodist process of interaction, education, and worship in communities across Mississippi.

Annual Convent Worship Services of Proclamation and Eucharist

In 2009, we planned the first service of preaching and Eucharist. The Episcopalians suggested the date: the Feast Day of John and Charles Wesley. I confess: We United Methodists wondered silently when that might be! It was revealed as the Episcopalians opened calendars to March. March 3 is the Feast Day of John and Charles Wesley, and we embraced this time in early March for the annual worship service. The host bishop would preside at Table, with the guest bishop preaching.

The expected quandary arose: wine or grape juice? We decided to use one loaf with two cups, the silver one containing wine and the pewter one containing grape juice. Three servants would offer the cup and bread at each station. The bread-bearer would stand in the middle, with the cupbearers on each side.

On March 3, 2009, Episcopalians and United Methodists gathered at Galloway United Methodist Church in Jackson at 5:30 for a delightful dinner together. The leaders of Galloway Church shared some of their long history, embodying United Methodist heritage. At 6:30, the two bishops led a procession down the street, around Smith Square, and into St. Andrew's Episcopal Cathedral for the service of worship. The texts appointed for the Feast Day are Isaiah 45:5–6 and Matthew 9:2–6: "I give you as light to the nations that my salvation may reach to the ends of the earth," and "Jesus sent the twelve out to proclaim the kingdom of God and to heal . . ."

The prayer for the feast day is written upon all our hearts: *Lord God, who inspired your servants John and Charles Wesley with burning zeal for the sanctification of souls, and endowed them with eloquence in speech and song: Kindle in your Church, we entreat you, such fervor, that those whose faith has cooled may be warmed, and those who have not known Christ may turn to him and be saved; who lives and reigns with you and the Holy Spirit, one God, now and forever. Amen.*

In the context of this grand service of worship, Bishop Gray and I placed our seals on two copies of the "Covenant of Life." The two Covenants were framed and placed in the offices of the two bishops. Prominent in my office to this day is a photograph taken in the midst of this service of worship. Copies of the covenant were distributed across our judicatories in the month of March.

It was a joyful, glorious evening of community, praise, and prayer. I emphasize the joyfulness of the occasion. Neighbors embraced one another, delighted to be in worship together, joyful to share in a bold and public witness of Christian unity.

The first week in March became for us the annual celebration of our covenant life. In 2010, the service was held in Meridian, with Episcopal Church of the Mediator hosting the worship service and United Methodists hosting a community gathering at the Meridian District Center afterward. In 2011, the service was held in Oxford, where our two parishes are in close proximity and our denominations have been in ministry together for many years. The congregation gathered at St. Peter's Episcopal Church for a reception and then processed to Oxford University United Methodist Church for the service of proclamation and Eucharist. In 2012, the service was held in Natchez at Grace United Methodist Church with a reception at Trinity Episcopal Church.

These services of worship and these times of community sharing were consistently joyful and glorious. Neighbors were delighted to worship together, to celebrate their common life in Christ and to simply be together. The experiences, each year, were profound and deep and rich. It is good to continue to meditate on the great joy in each gathering. Was the wellspring of joy from the simple reality of being together in unity with one another? Is there more to be learned from this as we continue in this journey toward unity?

Local Churches: Worship, Study, Pray, and Serve in Mission Together

We were very aware that many of our Episcopal and United Methodist Churches had longstanding and ongoing partnerships in the communities of our state. It was our hope to affirm these churches in the good work they were doing and to encourage others to connect and begin ministry within the covenant life of our denominations.

Anecdotally we heard many things. Churches shared the history of their shared mission outreach, work with children and youth, and worship traditions that included Holy Week services, Easter sunrise services, vacation Bible schools, youth ministries, and Thanksgiving services.

An Emergent Opportunity for Pastoral Ministry in Port Gibson

In the historic riverside community of Port Gibson, Episcopal and United Methodist laity began to envision shared ministry through their small neighboring churches. With their pastors, they articulated hope that their churches, in this community of economic and demographic decline, might partner in significant ways and share pastoral leadership.

The Episcopal and United Methodist pastors led conversations with the laity. They discerned that the time had come to ask their bishops to work together in providing clergy leadership in Port Gibson.

The United Methodist pastor serving the Port Gibson Church was approaching retirement and fully supported the ministry of his neighbor and colleague at the Episcopal Church.

Bishop Gray and I conferred, recognizing the wisdom of the clergy and laity in Port Gibson. We agreed on a plan forward. Bishop Gray affirmed the leadership of the Episcopal clergy for the two congregations. At the 2012 Annual Conference, it was my joy to appoint this Episcopal pastor to the Port Gibson Church.

Closing Reflection

The journey into the "Covenant of Life" in Mississippi and the journey within it were remarkable experiences of spiritual pilgrimage for us all.

We experienced unity in Christ, delighted in worship, grew in understanding and community, and reached out in mission.

We had the palpable sense of being faithful to a long and rich tradition of collaboration in Christian life and witness. As we met at the Duncan Gray Episcopal Retreat Center or at Millsaps College (United Methodist), at Episcopal churches and at United Methodist churches, we had the sense of standing on holy ground. Our horizons were pushed back, and our vision was expanded.

In Mississippi, in this season of our lives, God has been with us, leading us onward. We are grateful for the life we share in Christ.

Hope Morgan Ward is Bishop of the North Carolina Annual Conference. Prior to her appointment there in 2012, she served as Bishop of the Mississippi Annual Conference.

CHAPTER 11

A Time to Build Up

Phillip Duncan

This document is not the final chapter nor the last word in the relationship of and between the Episcopal Church and the United Methodist Church. It is an attempt to shed light on the relationship thus far between our two churches as we seek to deepen our commitment to this process of ecumenical sharing, while respecting and partnering each other's traditions as we grow closer in our working and ministering together. It is a continuation of personal, religious, social, and corporate relationships on many levels. It is a beginning for some and a time of joy and sorrow for others, as the work continues with new voices and faces around the table of hope and possibilities for a different relationship and a future that is still unfolding.

What lies ahead and how may we be called into deeper relationship within our two distinct and "cousin" churches? Over the last decade, the dialogue team comprised of members of the Episcopal Church and the United Methodist Church have met together, struggled, prayed, studied, shared, and been faithful in the task committed to us. The agenda was never to reach agreement on a proposal for a merger of our two communions, but rather to seek ways of sharing our faith and practice on a deeper level, recognizing our common heritage and our common affirmation of the Gospel and faith.

I have chosen to pull together strands of thoughts from others engaged in the dialogue conversations, and hope that the pastiche that is formed does justice to moving forward in the process. For all who have given themselves to this ecumenical dialogue, I give thanks to God.

The Episcopal Church states: "The mission of the Church is to restore all people to unity with God and each other in Christ."[1]

---

1 Book of Common Prayer, 855.

The United Methodist Church states: "The mission of the Church is to make disciples of Jesus Christ for the transformation of the world."[2] What we believe and celebrate as "gift" that we hold in common are:

- Our churches proclaim Jesus Christ as Lord and Savior.

- Our churches worship one God as the divine Trinity of Father, Son, and Holy Spirit; we baptize those who enter the Christian community in the name of the Father, Son and Holy Spirit.

- Our churches affirm the Holy Scriptures as "containing all things necessary for salvation," and as the primary rule for the life of the church.

- Our churches affirm and use the Nicene and Apostles' Creeds as sufficient summaries of the Christian faith.

- Our churches understand and practice the sacrament of Holy Baptism as initiation into the life of Christ through the church.

- Our churches understand and practice the sacrament of the Eucharist (Lord's Supper, Holy Communion, Divine Liturgy, Mass) as a means of divine grace that sustains and deepens our faith.

- Our churches continue to worship in ways that reflect our common liturgical and sacramental roots in our authorized liturgies.

- Our churches affirm the role of bishops as leaders of the life, work, and mission of the church, as symbols of unity, and as guiding and maintaining the church's apostolic faith and work.

- Our churches affirm the gifts and ministries of all persons as grounded in the grace given in baptism.

- Our churches have worked in the last half century to restore the office of deacon as a permanent order for servant ministry in the life of the church.

- Our churches affirm the need for prayer and holiness of heart and life, as ways of growth in the Christian faith.

- Our churches pursue social action and justice as inherent practices of Christian discipleship.

---

2 The Book of Discipline of the United Methodist Church, 2004, 87.

- Our churches affirm the unity of the church as the will of Christ for the sake of mission, service, and evangelism.

- Our churches affirm that the scriptures are to be understood today in the light of reasoned reflection on our contemporary experience.

The forgoing is not an exhaustive recounting; it is presented as informative. We need to view these common positions as touchstones, where we can continue deeper theological conversations and grapple together with both our common theology and our differences in theology. This needs to be engaged on all levels, including in the communities/congregations in which we live, within our gathered clergy groups, and with the laity. I believe that we need to engage how we "do church" and how we "are church," examining our practices (the enactment of our theology) to see how we live as faith communities. For the Episcopal Church, our understanding of *lex orandi, lex credendi* (praying what we believe; believing what we pray) needs to be more fully explicated.

Baptism for both the Episcopal Church and the United Methodist Church is understood within the process of Christian initiation. One enters the Christian community of faith, seeking to live into the Baptismal Covenant, which places study, prayer, amendment of life, commitment to Jesus Christ, and profession of faith within the overall process of growing into a deeper relationship with Christ and the gathered community, empowered to go into the world to live and proclaim the Gospel. What does "normative" imply to practice? Is it the same as "regular" or "required"? The canons of the Episcopal Church, the Anglican Communion, and a broad consensus of Christian tradition and practice have limited the sacrament of Holy Communion to those who have been baptized and can respond positively to the invitation given in the eucharistic liturgy. This issue is important and is foundational if Baptism is the rite of Christian initiation.

For the gathered community the Holy Eucharist is the central act of Sunday worship. How do we, together, continue/work to live into our declarations and statements upon which we base our deepening relationships? This is a challenge for both churches; it is our hope that as we develop and move forward, we do so honestly with questions and open hearts and minds, with one another. The Episcopal Church is challenged to seek broader balance between word and sacrament; understanding the presence of Christ is in the Word preached, the sacrament of the Body and Blood given and received, and the sending of the people gathered, back into the world for the mission of the Gospel. The

United Methodist Church is challenged to seek a balance of using the single cup upon the Holy Table and use wine (grape juice in a flagon) and bread, which following the people receiving the sacrament, any that is left over is disposed of reverently. That the sacrament of the Body and Blood is both sign and symbol, engages us in the meaning of "real presence" of Christ offered to the gathered people of God in bread broken and wine poured out. Are we able to live with and into mystery that is credible for us all?

The historic episcopate and conversations on this topic have been fulsome on both sides. For the Episcopal Church, the Chicago-Lambeth Quadrilateral (proposed by the House of Bishops of the Episcopal Church, 1886/1888) is foundational in moving forward: "The Historic Episcopate locally adapted in the methods of its administration to the varying needs of the nations and peoples called of God into the unity of His Church."[3] The reconciliation of the episcopacies of the United Methodist Church and the Episcopal Church are part of the ongoing work, study, and discussions, which we hope will bear fruit and lead to a process of shared ministries for both churches. In so doing, the opportunity for us together to affirm the following of our journey toward full communion must include a way to recognize and reconcile the two episcopacies in such a manner as not to call into question the authenticity of each other's ordinations. Both churches affirm the historic episcopate in the language of the "Baptism, Eucharist, and Ministry" statement, as a "sign," but not a guarantee, of the catholicity, unity, and continuity of the church.

- Both churches agree that the historic episcopate is always in a process of reform in the service of the Gospel.
- From their formative periods in the colonial age both churches locally adapted the historic episcopate for the sake of mission.
- We pray that we may move forward with respect for each other's gifts as we respect and engage each other's traditions.

The Episcopal Church understands that all ministry is grounded in Baptism. The ministries of trained and licensed laity are an important part of our common life together. The ministry of pastoral leader, worship leader, preacher, eucharistic minister, eucharistic visitor, evangelist, and catechist are important in the life of the various communities in which they serve. Each diocese has requirements for the training

---

3 Book of Common Prayer, 877.

of persons who exercise these specific ministries under the direction of an ordained clergy. Additionally, lay persons share in the governance of the church at the congregational level, diocesan level, and the national/international level in the General Convention. These positions are major and important for the well-being of the shared governance of the church.

The United Methodist Church affirms Baptism as the grounding for all ministry. In addition, there is a longstanding tradition of lay leaders teaching class, stewards, exhorters, preachers, lay pastors, and administrators leading congregations with worship, preaching, and, at times, presiding at Holy Communion. The lay presidency is a difficulty for the Episcopal Church, which has been addressed with the Evangelical Lutheran Church of America, with whom we are in full communion and which also licenses lay persons to preside at the Eucharist. The understanding is that such persons are not permitted to serve in the Episcopal Church and are not part of any formal recognition of ministries. It is our common belief that the licensed ministries for lay persons enrich our corporate lives. They offer services that otherwise would not be available and bring gifts that are treasures for us all in many Methodist and Episcopal congregations.

The issue of race and the sin of racism continues in both denominations as church-dividing. This is both internally within each of our churches as well as between Methodists and Episcopalians. It is our hope that as we continue to engage the issue of the sin of racism, we can learn in new ways how racism has and continues to wound the Body of Christ. Here is also an opportunity to move ahead in new and tangible ways to address this sin.

Both churches face the challenges of human sexuality and a growing international membership. Both of these challenges are opportunities to proclaim together the Good News of the Gospel for all people, and that in Christ there are no outcasts, only sisters and brothers to be welcomed into the community of faith. No one is disposable. In the current Interim Eucharistic Sharing agreement we are asked to seek ways to join together for common prayer, study, fellowship, and worship (both with and without Eucharist). This is a way forward. We continue our journey together as Methodists and Episcopalians. "Make us One in Christ" is our prayer as we move forward with open hearts, open minds and open hands to become the people of God. It is "a time to build up!"

Philip Duncan, Bishop of the Central Gulf Coast, is a member of the Episcopal-United Methodist Dialogue Team and chairs the Episcopal Church's Standing Committee on Ecumenism and Interreligious Relations.

CPSIA information can be obtained at www.ICGtesting.com
Printed in the USA
LVOW12s0450120414

381449LV00006B/6/P